My Shepherd
A Six-Week Devotional for Souls Longing for Green Pastures and Quiet Waters

John A. Matthews

JM Writing Press

To my amazing wife, Tonya, the love of my life;
To my cherished children, Alexander, Abigail, and Andrew,
who bring me such joy;
To my beloved parents, Matt and Alene, who raised me up in
the Lord;
I am so blessed by God.
To my Lord Jesus Christ, to Him be the glory forever.

♡♥♡♥

Contents

Introduction

P salm 23 has been an important passage of Scripture to me through the years. As a pastor, I have leaned on it during many seasons of loss and grief, and it has served as a faithful comfort and encouragement. It has provided direction as I have used it to mentor leaders and disciple young believers.

But I come to this familiar passage not only from a pastoral perspective but also from a fatherly one. Some years ago, as my children headed off to college, I undertook an endeavor to write them a devotional thought from time to time to continue to pour into their spiritual development, even as they moved out from under my roof to their own. So began the development of this book—a compilation and expansion of those devotions for my kids. I hope you can hear the heart of a dad as I seek to provide some insight and reflection for them.

The goal is to read through this psalm daily for the next six weeks. Monday through Friday have a devotional thought each day and some simple reflection questions that follow. On Saturday and Sunday, the challenge is to review the week's devotional and text and commit to memorizing a section of the psalm so that, at the end of the six weeks, you have the entire chapter committed to memory.

On Sunday, I encourage you to plug in to a local body of believers, the church. No church is perfect, but you and I are designed to walk through this journey of faith with other people. The church is where we find those fellow faith travelers. I understand there are an abundance of online options for church, and for some that is a necessity. However, for most of us, in-person gatherings are the best option, whether or not we like to admit it. Get plugged in. Grow in a community of other believers. There will be challenges and struggles as you go, but it is worth the journey.

May this book be a blessing for you, as it was for me. May God bless you as you discover the truth of the passage and can say, "The Lord is *My Shepherd*."

The LORD is my shepherd,
I shall not want.
He makes me lie down in green pastures;
He leads me beside quiet waters.
He restores my soul;
He guides me in the paths of righteousness
For His name's sake.
Even though I walk through the valley of the shadow of death,
I fear no evil, for You are with me;
Your rod and Your staff, they comfort me.
You prepare a table before me in the presence of my enemies;
You have anointed my head with oil;
My cup overflows.
Surely goodness and lovingkindness will follow me all the days
of my life,
And I will dwell in the house of the LORD forever.
Psalm 23:1–6

Week 1

The LORD is my shepherd.
Psalm 23:1

Week 1 Monday
The LORD is my shepherd.
Psalm 23:1

Over the course of my fifty years of life, I've been known by many different titles. I've been John the friend, John the student, John the teacher. People have known me as a coworker, classmate, supervisor, pastor, and counselor. Perhaps my favorite titles are John the husband and John the father. Each one of these titles speaks to the way I have related to someone. They are unique descriptors of personal relationships.

Not everyone can call me their classmate—only those who went to school with me.

While I try to be friendly to everyone, only a few can call me friend.

I am the husband of only one and the father to only three.

The name you call me is, by and large, based on the relationship we share.

Psalm 23 is one of my favorite passages of Scripture. It's not lengthy, but it is full of comfort, encouragement, and conviction.

David probably wrote this psalm while he was king, later in his life, making this passage around three thousand years old or so. By the time David had written this, he had had plenty of time to reflect on his relationship with God. He had seen the Lord move in powerful ways from the time of his youth when he faced a giant, to his experiences as a young man when God protected him as King Saul continually tried to kill him off, to the season when God led him as he became a king himself, to the moment of him writing this psalm.

There are lots of titles David could have called God and been entirely correct. God is my provider, God is my healer, God is my leader. Each of those would be true. But David settled on a title that I think really hit home for him. It was a name that had profound meaning for him. It was a name that spoke of a special relationship he knew well.

The Lord is *My Shepherd*.

David knows a thing or two about shepherds. While shepherds were common in that day and area, David is especially familiar with what a shepherd is. After all, he not only saw shepherds, but he had also been a shepherd himself. He knows the special relationship between a shepherd and his sheep. He understands the protection and care that a good shepherd provides to the sheep under his watch. When David looks at his life and the continual care that the Lord has poured over his life, he relates it to a familiar image—that of a shepherd caring for his sheep.

The Lord is the Shepherd. David is the sheep.

This psalm flows out of David's understanding of his special relationship with the Lord. Of all the titles David could have called the Lord, *this* is the one in this moment of his life that fits best. And while it is special, it is neither unique nor exclusive to David. All those who have trusted in Jesus can enjoy what we'll observe in this psalm. While there are a lot of ways you can identify with the Lord today, let's start with seeing Him as *your Shepherd*.

Let's take some time to dig into what that means for you and me to say the Lord is *My Shepherd*.

Questions for Today:

1. What titles are you known by, and what do they say about the relationships you hold?

2. What are some ways you relate to God? If you were to give Him a title based on your current relationship, what would it be?

3. When you think about shepherd imagery, what immediately comes to mind? Where do those thoughts spring from?

4. How would knowing God as your Shepherd impact the way you face life's challenges this week?

Prayer for Today:

Lord, thank You for Your personal relationship with me. Thank You for being a God who loves me and chooses to be up close and personal in my life. Today, help me see You as the Shepherd of my life. Lead me toward where You want me to go. Guide my thoughts and my steps as I seek to be obedient to You. I may not have it all together quite yet but continue to mold me into what You created me to be. To You be the glory.

Amen.

Week 1 Tuesday
The LORD is my shepherd.
Psalm 23:1

For us to say that the Lord is our Shepherd, it requires that we make an important admission. If He is our Shepherd, that must mean we are His sheep.

If you think about it for a second, that really isn't a compliment for us.

We aren't lions.

We're not bears.

We don't even get to be tigers.

No, we are simply sheep.

Sheep unjustly get a bad rap. People often think of them as dumb animals. True, we don't recognize sheep because of their intelligence. However, what distinguishes them is their trust in someone who can see dangers they cannot. David and others are trying to point out that it isn't their ignorance that marks them; it is their dependence. Sheep are totally reliant on the care of the shepherd. If they want to survive, they need the help of a loving shepherd.

When attacked, sheep don't put up much of a fight. The sheep are easy prey for their predators, both thieves and wolves. They have no natural defense mechanisms, no razor-sharp teeth, no terrifying claws, no high-speed maneuverability. They don't even have a menacing voice.

No growl or howl. Just baaaa.

Without a shepherd to fend off the enemy, the sheep are going to be a quick-service meal for somebody.

While threats from outside are a constant danger for the sheep, it is also true that sheep are a danger to themselves. Sheep have a bad habit of wandering off and have no real sense of direction. They may be in a nice green pasture, but if left unattended, they will wander off and starve. They get caught in thickets, stuck and unable to get out. I've even heard it said that sheep can fall in such a way, on their backs with their legs in the air, that without a shepherd to right them, they cannot get back up. The flock will move on, and the sheep will just lie there helplessly and ultimately die.

We could go on, but I think you get the picture. The shepherd's care directly affects a sheep's health and well-being.

You and I are those sheep. Psalm 100:3 says, "We are His people and the sheep of His pasture." Throughout Scripture, God's people are called His sheep. Isaiah 53:6 reminds us that being a sheep means we, too, tend to go astray. "All of us like sheep have gone astray, each of us has turned to his own way."

We wander off. We find ourselves in places we never intended to be, caught up in the briers of our own poor choices. Somehow, we got into this bind but can't figure out how to escape it. The enemy attacks us, seeking to rob us of our joy and peace, seeking to devour us. While we want to put up a fight, the reality is, we are powerless by ourselves against the assault. We leave the green pastures and can't figure out why we are spiritually starving.

Though we may be sheep, thank goodness we have a Good Shepherd! You may find yourself in a hard place, but the Shepherd will not leave you there. Look up and see Him. The enemy may come at you hard. The Shepherd is there to protect you. Trust the Shepherd. Whether you're caught in the thicket, have wandered off to a dry pasture, or are being assailed by some wolf, let the Shepherd rescue you. Our problem is that we think we can get out of it ourselves. If we just try harder, do better, pray more, then we can get ourselves out of the mess we find ourselves in. We resist submitting to the Shepherd and just keep kicking in a futile effort to rescue ourselves. But it never works. Sheep need the Shepherd's care. Wherever you find yourself, stop kicking against Him and let Him carry you to where you need to be. Let Him place you back in that green pasture. He is the Good Shepherd. *You* are just a sheep.

Take some time to consider how you see that relationship dynamic expressed in your life.

Questions for Today:

1. What are some ways that you are like a sheep? What thickets have you found yourself in?

2. How have you seen God act as Shepherd in your life?

3. Is there a direction that you have wandered that has taken you from green pastures to a parched soul?

4. In what ways do you need to submit to the Shepherd's care?

Prayer for Today:

Thank You, Lord, for Your care over my life. I haven't always gone the way I should; I have tended to wander. I have, of my own choosing, wandered to places I should have never gone. But You have never given up on me. You continue to pursue me and rescue me both from outside attacks and from my own destructive tendencies. Thank You for Your love and care for me, Your sheep. Help me listen and follow my Shepherd more each day.

Amen.

Week 1 Wednesday
The Lord is my shepherd.
Psalm 23:1

E veryone has secrets, things that no one else knows. At least
they think they do.

Some years ago, late one Saturday night, I ran a stop sign that
was located in front of my high school. I knew I should have
stopped, but nobody was around. I was in a hurry, and who'd
notice, anyway?

Hardly even a mile down the road, I saw some headlights
coming up quickly behind me. I remember thinking, "Man,
they sure are in a hurry. They'd better be careful not to get a
ticket!"

And that's when the blue lights came on. They were in a
hurry, all right! They were in fast pursuit of a knucklehead who
thought nobody would notice a car running a stop sign late at
night.

Thankfully, the officer was kind enough to let me off with
just a warning. No one saw me pulled over, I didn't get a ticket,
and there was no chance that my parents would ever find out. I
was feeling pretty confident. I dodged a bullet, for sure.

That all changed at church the next morning. I struck up a
conversation with a close friend of my parents. She seemed to
have a strange interest in the events of the previous evening. She
asked curious questions about whether I had had any unusual
adventures the night before. Then it hit me; she was a 911

dispatcher. When the officer had taken my license to run it, she had heard my name over the radio!

I was busted.

It was not so secret anymore.

It's nice to think that there are parts of our lives that only we know about. However, we are known more than we think. I'm not naive enough to believe that I know everything that my kids, my friends, or others do. But I am also smart enough to know that even though I may not know every detail of their lives, there is One who does. Nothing is ever really hidden.

The important thing we need to remember is this: The Lord is our Shepherd. We are His sheep. The Shepherd knows His sheep.

Jesus, fully aware of Psalm 23, takes up the imagery of the Lord as the Shepherd. In John 10, Jesus identifies Himself as the Good Shepherd, inserting Himself into the picture described in the psalm. As Jesus talks, He reminds those listening about an important aspect of shepherding life—shepherds know their sheep. Jesus says in verse 3 that good shepherds know their sheep so well that they can call the sheep out by name. Out of all the sheep, the shepherd knows which is which. In John 10:14, Jesus says, "I am the good shepherd, and I know My own." Jesus knows His sheep.

Throughout Jesus's ministry, you see plenty of evidence that He knows people. Scripture reveals Jesus was aware of what people were thinking and what was in their heart. He knew what kind of life they were living before ever even speaking to them. In a broad sense, Jesus had people figured out better than they had themselves figured out.

Consider for a moment the depth of what Jesus knows about you. As God eternal, Jesus has full insight into your life. Read Psalm 139 and brace yourself. The Lord knows when you get up and when you go to bed, and He knows everything that you do in-between. He knows your thoughts and motivations and knows the words you speak before they even come out of your mouth. He knows where you've been, where you are, and where you're going. You can't run from Him, and there's nowhere you can hide from Him. He sees the end of your journey just as clearly as He sees the beginning. He knows you completely. No secrets, nothing hidden, nothing in your life unknown.

Now that should partly terrify you. Right? He knows *everything*. There are some things that we wish He hadn't seen or didn't know. Let's be real. Not every action we engage in is honorable. Not every thought is pure. Not every motivation is clean. Not every word is appropriate for public consumption or suitable for company. Being aware that He sees and knows it all can bring with it a bit of fear and trembling, and rightly so.

We try to hide the less than pleasant areas of our lives. We hide out in the shadows hoping He won't see, or we try to run from Him, afraid of what will happen if He really knows the true us. But He already knows. He always has. He knows *you*. And He still wants to shepherd you. The Shepherd knows what you struggle with and what your strengths and weaknesses are. He knows your circumstances, your opportunities, and your limitations. He knows what you're passionate about, and He knows what tempts you to wander. He understands better than anyone what makes you tick. He knows everything about you.

The Good Shepherd is calling the names of His sheep. He knows what they need because He knows them. He desires to lead them toward exactly what they need. Blessing. Joy. Growth. Satisfaction. After all, He says in John 10:10 that He came so that His sheep might have life to the fullest! He is calling them by name, leading them to where they need to go.

The Shepherd is calling your name. He knows what makes you tick and what will bring you life.

Hear Him call.

Follow the Shepherd who knows you.

Questions for Today:

1. When you think of what Jesus knows about you, how does that make you feel?

2. What are some things you are glad He knows?

3. What are some things you wish He didn't know?

4. How would your life be different if you lived in the realization that Jesus is fully aware of every aspect of your life?

5. How does His knowledge of you affect how He can

lead you to what you really need?

Prayer for Today:

Thank You, Lord, for Your complete awareness of my life. You created me, You know me, and You love me. Let me rest in the assurance of both Your infinite knowledge of my life and Your unceasing care over my life. Thank You for offering grace and forgiveness when I stumble, patience as I often wander, and compassion when I refuse to listen to Your voice as I should. Help me hear the voice of my Shepherd and follow His voice today.

Amen.

Week 1 Thursday
The LORD is my shepherd.
Psalm 23:1

When you love someone, you will go to incredible lengths to take care of them. You will go to the ends of the earth and back to make sure they are okay.

The phone rang one afternoon. Abby, my daughter, was on the other end of the line. Panic was in her voice; I was ready to jump to respond. She had hit a pothole, had a flat, and was now stuck on the side of the road. Help!

This wasn't across town; she was at college. It would require at least a forty-five-minute drive there, time fixing the tire, and then the return trip back home. This was an unscheduled interruption of my day.

Did I hesitate for one second to go? Not a chance. You respond when people you love are in need.

When I arrived on the scene, it wasn't one flat tire; it was two. Both complete blowouts. It was more than a simple tire change. Did I hesitate for one second to get her off the road and to safety? Not a chance! You take care of the people you love.

Years later, a call came out of the blue. A despair-filled voice asked, "Dad, will you come get me? I need to come home." Thousands of miles separated us. No hesitation. I jumped on a flight, and I was there to be right where she needed me to be. For those you love, you love not just in words but in action.

The shepherd cares for his sheep.

We're not talking about mere sentimentality or simple affection.

We're not talking about a warm, fuzzy feeling.

No, we are talking about a kind of love and care that is expressed through blood, sweat, and tears.

Being a shepherd isn't easy or for the faint of heart. Shepherding is hard work. You've got the sheep to deal with. Stubborn sheep don't want to go in the direction that is healthy for them. Sheep get injured and beat up and need to be picked up, cleaned up, and bandaged up. The sheep may not like it, appreciate it, or sometimes even yield willingly to it, but the shepherd does what is in the best interest of the sheep so that they can thrive and grow.

But the sheep aren't the only challenge.

There are predators that want to hurt the sheep, and as we've said, sheep can't fight for themselves. The shepherd has to fight off wolves and other animals wanting to devour the sheep. Snarling teeth aren't just directed at the sheep; these predators snap at the shepherd too. Would you want to volunteer to have an angry wolf with an enormous appetite come at you as you stood between them and their lunch? No? A good shepherd stands his ground and chases off all those that threaten his sheep.

There are thieves and bandits who want to steal the sheep for their own benefit. They don't care about the sheep; they only care about what the sheep can gain for them. They see the sheep for its wool, for food, or for the money they can pocket by selling it to someone else. These robbers, as it says in John 10:10, just want to kill and destroy. A good shepherd is ready to defend the sheep. No thief is going to harm them on his watch. Running away from the fight isn't an option.

Caring for sheep comes at a cost, but the good shepherd will pay it.

Read John 10:11–15. Not every person meets the requirements to be a good shepherd. When the attackers come, some want none of it. They take off and leave the sheep to fend for themselves. We all know people like that. We've all had friends who are here for us when times are great, but as soon as there is conflict, leave us high and dry. Or we've had teammates who give their all when you are winning, but when the losses pile up, they pack it up and quit. When things get tough, some people rise up and others run off. The good shepherd doesn't go anywhere when conflict comes. While the hired hand cares about himself, the good shepherd cares for his sheep.

You've had people abandon you when you needed them. You were going through a tough time, and all those friends you thought you had were nowhere to be found. The storm winds were blowing, the waves were crashing on you, and you were struggling to stay afloat. You looked around, and those you relied on were missing in action.

But you were not alone; the Good Shepherd was there. He was still caring for you, even though you may not have seen Him at that moment. If you are His sheep, He isn't going anywhere.

He will stick by you, protect you, and lead you even when, or maybe *especially* when, times are tough.

We aren't always easy to care for. We wander, we resist, we think we can figure it out on our own. The Good Shepherd, Jesus, sticks with you and me. Even when we kick against Him, He still gently guides us in the direction we need to go. He cares deeply for us.

When things get messy, when we find ourselves in the thickets and briers of our own hardheadedness, He still reaches in and pulls us out, cleans us up, and puts us on the right path again. He won't abandon us. Even if everyone else does.

The enemy continues to attack. The devil seeks to rob your joy, steal your blessing, and discourage your walk. He would love to see you defeated and destroyed. The Good Shepherd is on your side. He is protecting you with His mighty right hand. You can rest easy knowing that the Good Shepherd stands between you and the enemy, and He will not let him get to you.

Rest today in the assurance of His care for you.

Questions for Today:

1. What is a way that you have seen Jesus care for you?

2. When was a time you saw others run away when your life got messy?

3. How does it feel knowing that the Good Shepherd will

always stay with you?

4. How can you live considering that awareness today?

Prayer for Today:

Thank You, Lord, for Your constant care over my life. I am not always easy to deal with. I can be stubborn and hardheaded and can get myself into a mess without too much trouble. I am prone to wandering. Yet You never leave me to fight my own battles. Help me today to yield to Your care as I know that You have my best interest at heart.

Amen.

The Lord is my shepherd.
Psalm 23:1

W hy does the Good Shepherd do what He does? Why does He keep on dealing with obstinate sheep like us? Why does He continue to pursue sheep that prefer to wander in their own direction?

The answer is quite simple: love.

The Shepherd loves His sheep.

We spend so much time searching for love. Unfortunately, too often, we end up settling for a knock-off version of true love—a cheap imitation of the real thing. You can buy Ray-Ban sunglasses for $10 on the street corners of NYC. They look real enough, but upon close examination, they are more like Roy-Buns. They may look good at first but never hold up to much wear.

We want to be accepted. We want to be loved unconditionally. But that type of love is hard to find. The love we see naturally in the world around us comes with a "what have you done for me lately" tag on it. We keep searching for the love that will satisfy and bring fulfillment, but all we find is a love that is self-serving and selfish.

Is it any wonder that the journey to find love leaves so many heartbroken and disappointed?

There is a love that is real, and it seeks to be found. It's a love that is the very opposite of self-serving. It's sacrificial. There's a love that isn't contingent on what we bring to the table, and we don't earn it by being exceptional. It is freely available but found only in one place.

I love going to New York City. I may be a small-town guy, but there is something about that city that captivates me. The sights, the sounds all pull me in. One of my favorite places to go in New York City is the Empire State Building. The experience of traveling to the recently renovated and upgraded observation deck and looking out over the city is a highlight every time. When I travel to New Orleans, I can look for that observation deck, but I will not find it there. If I head over to Orlando, I can see the Mouse, but I will not find the Empire State Building. There is only one place to get the view from the Empire State Building, and that is in New York City. Why travel to Boston, Chicago, Dallas, or Memphis to look for something that I know is only found at 350 Fifth Avenue, New York, New York? It would be silly to look for something where you know it can't be found.

You can find genuine love only in one place. We find it in the Good Shepherd. The Shepherd loves His sheep. How do we know? Jesus says so. He says the Shepherd (who He says He is) lays down His life for His sheep. Now let's look at the big picture here. Jesus says just a few chapters over in John 15 that there is no greater love than one laying down his life for his friends. And that is exactly what Jesus does! He sacrifices His very life for His friends, *and* He says we are His friends.

Think about two verses that you may already know. John 3:16 tells us, "For God so loved the world that He gave His only begotten Son, that whoever believes in Him shall not perish, but have eternal life."

Romans 5:8 says it this way, "But God demonstrates His own love toward us, in that while we were yet sinners, Christ died for us."

God writes His love for us in blood-red letters. We are sheep that wander astray, and the Shepherd laid down His life for us. He loves us so much that He was willing to give His own life so that we can live. The Good Shepherd laid down His life for His sheep; He laid down His life for you. Why? Because He loves you that much.

You'll always be tempted to chase after a love that never satisfies. You can pursue all the relationships and pleasures this world offers and yet never be fulfilled. Cheap imitations of the real thing easily fool us. But why keep on searching for it in places it cannot be found? There is an unconditional and sacrificial love that calls out to you today. It is in the arms of the Good Shepherd.

I love what Isaiah says in Isaiah 40:11, "Like a shepherd He will tend His flock, In His arm He will gather the lambs And carry them in His bosom; He will gently lead the nursing ewes."

What a magnificent picture! Jesus, the Good Shepherd, carrying you, His sheep, close to His heart. It's an amazing image of the care and love of the Shepherd for His sheep. As you reflect on this truth today, I hope you enjoy the care that He desires to provide you.

The Lord is my Shepherd . . .

Questions for Today:

1. What are some places you have looked to find love?

2. How has that search left you feeling?

3. What is a way that you have seen God's unconditional love toward you?

4. How does it make you feel to consider that God loves you as much when you are at your worst as He does when you are at your best?

5. In what ways do we sometimes find ourselves chasing the imitations instead of the true love expressed by the Good Shepherd?

Prayer for Today:

Thank You, Lord, for loving me and for never giving up on me. Thank You for dying for me. I didn't earn it or deserve it, but You freely gave Your life for me. May I live today in appreciation for the sacrifice given on my behalf. Help me love others in a manner that reflects Your love toward me.

Amen.

Week 1 Saturday and Sunday
The Lord is my shepherd.
Psalm 23:1

G o back and review the questions from this week's daily devotions.

1. How has this week's theme of the Lord being our Shepherd affected how you view your relationship with God?

2. What is one aspect of the shepherd/sheep dynamic that encouraged you this week?

3. What is something in your walk with the Lord you will change in response to this week's devotion?

4. Commit the first line of Psalm 23:1 to memory: "The Lord is my shepherd."

Find a family of faith (church) and get plugged in! As followers of Jesus, we are created to be part of the body of Christ. Join other believers to worship the Good Shepherd.

Week 2

I shall not want. He makes me lie down in green pastures; He leads me beside quiet waters.

Psalm 23:1–2

I have a lot of wants. Ever since I was old enough to drive, if not before then, I have longed for one particular car. It's not just any car, either; it is *the* car . . . a 1965 Ford Mustang. Through the years, I've seen quite a few. I've even driven one. But as I left the house this morning, there still wasn't one sitting in my driveway. Make no mistake. I want one. Badly. Cherry red with a stick shift would be phenomenal. But thirty-plus years now into my dream, I still don't have it.

I may never.

That's just one *want* I have. There are plenty of others too. I *want* to have a bank account where I have to worry about FDIC limits. I *want* all the leaves raked up in my yard before I have to do it. I *want* the weight to magically fall off so I don't have to worry about exercise or eating right.

Seems like a lot of my *wants* never materialize.

Truthfully, we all have *wants*. Some more serious than others. We *want* lasting relationships, friendships that go beyond just the surface level, job stability, good health reports. We *want* to know people care about us. We *want* to know we can put a meal on the table. We *want* to be able to pay the bills. We *want* to not stress out over life.

The claim the psalmist makes in Psalm 23:1 is pretty incredible. It is this: Since the Lord is our Shepherd, we will *want* for nothing.

How then do we reconcile that claim with the reality of our *wanting* lives?

The key is understanding what *want* is. Perhaps that word doesn't mean what we think it does.

When we say *want,* what we mean is, what we desire. It is our extensive list of things we wish we had. Like making out a Christmas list for Santa, some of those wants get pretty elaborate and extensive. After all, why not ask for those brand-new kicks if you really *want* them? If you really desire that new job, why not expect God to give it to you? However, if we aren't careful, we can twist this verse into making God our own personal genie. Give the command, and He will snap His fingers, and your *want* is provided for! Seems fair enough. In fact, you can even find some religious people who say that is exactly how God works. If you believe and have enough faith, God will give you everything you *want*—good health, fat bank accounts, worldly possessions, you name it!

Here is the thing. That's not how it works! A read-through of the Bible throws that theory out the window real quick. God is not a genie. He is our Shepherd.

In Psalm 23, *want* doesn't mean desires. The Hebrew word here means to be lacking. In Deuteronomy, *want* describes God's people's condition as they wandered in the wilderness. In Deuteronomy 2:9, Moses reminds the people that they wandered around for forty years, but they lacked nothing they needed. God always provides. Every time you chase the word down in Scripture, *want* describes something that is run out of, missed out on, or lacking. If that is the meaning elsewhere, it likely has the same meaning in the Psalms. So here in Psalms, David is saying that because the Lord is our shepherd, we lack for nothing. It is more closely related to our needs and not our desires. The Shepherd constantly cares for us and therefore we lack nothing. So, we can say it this way: If the Lord is our Shepherd, we will have everything we need.

The challenge for us is to understand the difference between desires and needs. We can trust that the Shepherd is always providing for our needs, even if a '65 Mustang is never parked in the driveway.

As you start a new week, consider how the Shepherd continually provides for the needs of His sheep.

Questions for Today:

1. If you were to make a list, how would you differentiate between what your wants are and what your needs are?

2. What do you see as your top five needs in your life right now?

3. How do you see God's hand at work providing for those needs?

4. How do you typically respond when you have a need, and God has not yet provided for it?

Prayer for Today:

Thank You, Lord, for being a caring Shepherd who knows me and provides for every need I have. Help me trust You and be patient as You are meeting those needs on Your timetable and not my own. Help me discern between what I desire and what I truly need. Let me live daily in the assurance of Your continual provision for my life.

Amen.

Week 2 Tuesday
I shall not want.
Psalm 23:1

As I've gotten older, how I view what I really need has changed. When I was younger, my needs always felt so tangible. I could point at them or put my hands on them. It was a specific object, a certain relationship, or a particular happening. I need *that*. Funny thing is, when I got *that*, I still didn't have what I really needed. Or stranger still, when I didn't get *that*, I still found I had what I needed. In seasons when I thought I had more than enough and seasons when I thought I had nothing, I have always found I have had exactly what I need.

I remember years ago when Tonya and I were newlyweds. We were in seminary, working full time at part-time pay and had plenty of bills to pay. We were sinking. Money was tight. Okay, there was no money. It was a major challenge trying to figure out how we were going to make it through the month with no money coming in and too much money needing to go out. We had a plan. We had some antiques that we would sell to a local antique shop. It made perfect sense to us. It was the perfect plan God was going to use to provide for our needs.

Except He didn't provide for the needs that way.

I still remember the guy in the shop laughing at the stuff we brought in. Or maybe he was laughing at us. Either way, he wasn't interested.

Do you know how God provided for us instead?

No?

Me either. I just know He did. I don't know how God provided what He did. I just know He always provided what we needed. Somehow, the bills always got paid each month, and we never went hungry. We were never in *want*.

There was another season early in married life when things were tight. I just knew we were going under. This time, an unexpected letter came in the mail. It was a simple card from some relatives that said they loved us and wanted to bless us. In it was a check that covered the amount we needed at that very moment. They didn't know what we were going through, but God did.

Sometimes God intervenes miraculously to take care of a problem I have. Sometimes when I expect Him to show up and show out, I can't see Him do anything at all. Yet, in both situations, I have always had everything I needed. I may not be as comfortable sometimes, but I have never lacked.

Paul in Philippians 4:10–19 talks about something similar. He says that sometimes he has had an abundance—he has lived in prosperity. There have been other times when he has had very little. He's experienced a full belly and lived hungry too. But he says that he has always had what he needed in order to do what God called him to do. In this context, in saying he's been to both extremes, he gladly proclaims, with whatever he has, "I can do all things through Him who strengthens me!" (Philippians 4:13). How is that possible? Well, he answers that himself in verse 19. "And my God will supply all your needs, according to His riches in glory in Christ Jesus." Through Jesus, you'll always have enough. We may not have all our selfish desires, but we'll never be in *want*. We lack for nothing we need.

Sometimes the shepherd will dramatically rescue the sheep. He'll pull them out of a thicket or save them from a wolf. A lot of times, though, it's just the steady leadership of the shepherd that provides for the needs of the sheep, leading the sheep to a better place, helping them avoid the thickets and wolves altogether. Some needs are obvious; others are unknown even to the sheep, but the shepherd knows. The Good Shepherd faithfully cares for His sheep. They don't have to be anxious. They just need to trust and follow their Shepherd.

Look for ways the Lord provides for you today. It may not be how you expect!

Questions for Today:

1. When was a time you thought God was going to do something in a certain way, only to see that He responded differently?

2. Looking back, was there a time God met a need that you didn't think He was meeting at the time?

3. What were some needs you had that later you found were not needs at all?

4. What does it mean to you when Paul says that God provides for our needs "according to His riches in glory in Christ Jesus?"

Prayer for Today:

Lord, let me walk after You in assurance. I know You and trust You to care for my every need. Not every need I have is what I think it is. You know me, Your sheep, and You know what I truly need. Help me rely on You, trusting You see what is best for me. Thank You for those moments You show out in a big way, miraculously providing for me. Thank You for the many moments unseen by my human eyes where You provide for me, and I can't yet see it. Give me eyes more open to observe Your hand at work in my life and Your constant provision.

Amen.

Week 2 Wednesday
He makes me lie down in green pastures;
He leads me beside quiet waters.
Psalm 23:2

On their sixteenth birthdays, I took my sons and hiked the Grand Canyon. Two different trips, two different years, but the same goal. I have taken both Alex and Andrew, making memories along the way with both as a rite of passage, a march into manhood.

Alex and I had planned our route and schedule in advance. We were to hike all the way to the canyon floor on day one and then split up the return ascent into the following two days.

When we began, it was nice and cool. We both even had on windbreakers to warm us up just a bit. It was late July, so the fact that the temperature was so mild was quite encouraging.

Then we descended into Hades. The more we hiked, the hotter it got. By the time we reached the canyon floor, the temperature was approximately the same as the surface of the sun. At least it *felt* like it.

It had been a challenging hike. We had made reservations to stay at a primitive camping area just across the Colorado River. We crossed over and set up camp at a quiet campground next to Bright Angel Creek.

By the time we arrived at our destination, the journey had worn us out completely. We were absolutely exhausted. Thirsty. Drained of all energy.

When we approached the Colorado River, it was mighty tempting to jump in. When sweat drenches your body, your legs are aching, and you are hot and tired, the water looks so inviting. But even delirious from the sun and the hike, we thought the better of getting in. The water was too cold and the current too swift for us. In our exhausted state, it would not have been a wise decision to get in.

However, the creek at the campground was a different story. It was just right!

We jumped in with full clothes on and sat down in the middle of the calmly flowing creek. It was perfect! The water cooled us off and refreshed us just like we needed. It was worth the wait.

At one time or another, we've all experienced the cool refreshment that only water can provide. Whether it was a glass of ice-cold water when you were thirsty, a jump into the lake or pool when it was so hot outside, or playing in the sprinkler when you were a kid. Water refreshes!

Here in verse 2 of Psalm 23, David reminds us of the satisfaction and refreshment the Good Shepherd brings His sheep. He leads them beside the quiet waters.

Sometimes it can feel like the journey to get to those waters is long and difficult.

It is important to note some details. The shepherd leads the sheep to just the *right* water. Sheep aren't excellent swimmers. If it were a raging river that the sheep wandered to, the water wouldn't refresh them; it would sweep them away! Sheep can't thrive in a stagnant pool either. That kind of water is unhealthy.

The quiet waters are slow-moving streams that allow the sheep to stand and drink safely. They experience the cool, refreshing waters without fear or struggle. These sheep, who have been grazing all day in the scorching sun, now have a place to be refreshed. The shepherd sees to it.

Your Shepherd wants your soul's thirst to be quenched, so He leads you to a place where you can find full satisfaction. He wants you to be refreshed. The best part is, He is the refreshment. Jesus calls Himself the Living Water, and you can be sure that He brings the satisfaction your soul craves.

Let the cool waters the Good Shepherd leads you to refresh your thirsty soul today.

Questions for Today:

1. When was a time you were extremely thirsty, and in what ways did that affect you?

2. Can you think of a time when your spirit was thirsty? What did you do to quench that thirst?

3. How does the image of the sheep being led to quiet waters relate to how you feel today? Are you still thirsting, or is your thirst being satisfied?

Prayer for Today:

Lord, lead me to the cool, quiet waters so that You can refresh my soul and quench my thirst. Help me not to drink from the sources that are unhealthy and unfruitful to me. Today, whatever comes my way, let me find my satisfaction in You.

Amen.

Week 2 Thursday
He makes me lie down in green pastures;
He leads me beside quiet waters.
Psalm 23:2

As part of a school trip, the whole family loaded up in a charter bus headed for Walt Disney World. Excitedly, we were driving through the night to arrive at the park by the time it opened the next day. Alex was old enough to be sitting with friends in a different part of the bus or on another bus entirely. But the youngest, Andrew, stayed close by. Sitting behind his mother and me, next to his sister, he was prepared for the journey. We had purchased snacks for him—enough for the entire trip. So, there he was, settled in with ample snacks, his favorite stuffed animal, electronic device in hand to keep him distracted . . . the works. We tucked him in nicely in a comfy blanket, ready for the multiple-hour trek to the most magical place on earth.

Things were going well for a few hours . . .

Then, things took a turn for the worse.

First came the sound. The unmistakable sound of some poor child getting violently ill. Then came the realization that the "some child" was, in fact, *our* child. And he was *very* ill. I'll save you the gruesome details, but let's just say his clothes, shoes, blanket, and favorite stuffed animal did not survive that night's ride.

Panic set in. Was it the dreaded stomach bug?

Car sickness?

What was it?

About that time, we came to an important confession/discovery. What we found out was that he had been eating those snacks. More specifically, he had eaten *all* his snacks. Snacks for the entire week had been consumed in a matter of an hour or so. He inhaled all the gummy worms, chips, crackers, you name it, at record speed. It filled him up good, but it was not good. We all reaped the consequences.

Filling up on just anything is not beneficial; in fact, it can be harmful. Unfortunately, we don't always do a good job of differentiating between the good stuff and junk. Thankfully, we have One who leads us to what will fill us and not the stuff that makes us sick.

Just as the shepherd leads the flock across the hillsides, the Good Shepherd leads us to places where we can graze and find nourishment. Sheep won't naturally find those spots. They need the shepherd to get them there. Those dry, rocky hillsides don't look like they'd be home to good food, but the shepherd knows better.

You'll always find yourself tempted to graze in areas that aren't good for you. There are areas that seem like they're fruitful but will just make you sick. When we start feasting on what we think will satisfy us rather than what the Shepherd is leading us to, we may find our appetite quenched but only for a moment. Pretty soon, the bellyache (and often heartache) hit with ferocity.

Before we think about what the junk is, let's consider what the good food is. For us, the source of our nourishment is the Word of God. We find that the more we feed on it, the stronger we are.

First Peter 2:2 says, "Like newborn babies, long for the pure milk of the word, so that by it you may grow in respect to salvation." Nourishment, and therefore growth, comes through our feeding on the Word of God. The more we chew on it, the healthier we are. There is a definite connection between feeding on the Word and not lacking anything we need. Our *wants* are answered through the green pastures.

God continues to speak to us through His Word. That begs the question: How much of it are we regularly feeding on? He is providing wisdom, insight, and direction as we graze on it. Unfortunately, the Shepherd leads many sheep to the green pasture, but they refuse to eat. They're sure they'll figure it out on their own, but seldom actually do. They end up spiritually starving when the food is right in front of them. If the Shepherd leads you to a good place to graze, don't pass up the opportunity. He has you there for a reason; He knows what you need to feed on. Eat up.

Questions for Today:

1. How often are you feeding on the Word of God?

2. How can you make regular Bible study an active part

of your life?

3. What has been your experience meditating on the Word of God? What helps or hinders this experience?

4. Can you think of ways you can increase your appetite for the Word?

Prayer for Today:

Thank You, Lord, for leading me to places where I can grow in You and where You provide me with all that I need to face each day. Help me follow and eat. Increase my appetite for Your Word! Don't let me fill up on junk that won't truly satisfy me.

Amen.

Week 2 Friday
He makes me lie down in green pastures;
He leads me beside quiet waters.
Psalm 23:2

The Good Shepherd is leading you toward what will nourish and refresh your soul. He is getting you to the places where you can have satisfaction, find peace, grow, and find blessing. But you must choose what to do as He leads you there.

Some sheep are stubborn and will not eat in the pasture or drink from the quiet waters. Even when the text says that He "makes me lie down," it isn't in the sense of He forces you. You've heard the phrase, "You can lead a horse to water, but you can't make him drink." Well, the same is true with sheep. "Makes me lie down" here is more akin to "settles us down in." The Shepherd gets us to where we need to be—the places that we could not find on our own. He leads us to the area where the grass grows and the water runs gently. We choose what we do when we get there.

Don't be a stubborn sheep.

Too often, rather than take advantage of what God has placed in front of us, we'd rather try to find satisfaction on our own in places where we'll never find it. Instead of grazing on the green grass, we'd prefer to eat trash and rocks. We think it's going to fill us up, but it never does.

I have a friend who said the same thing every time he began a relationship. "This is the one."

Every time.

There were a lot of "the ones."

He was sure that each relationship was going to be the one that brought him happiness; each girl was going to be the one who brought him fulfillment. He was wrong. A lot.

We are all like that from time to time. We are no different from him. Instead of the green field, he thought he was going to find nourishment in a different spot. We do the same. Each of us fills our lives up with stuff, hoping that it will complete us, but it never does. So, we keep chasing. Some people think they will find satisfaction in relationships. They think that intimacy with someone, emotionally or physically, will provide what they are missing. Others turn to substances. They drink, smoke, shoot up, all with the same hope that maybe this will fill the emptiness they experience. Some turn to busyness. They keep running and doing. Maybe in the pursuit of everything, they can at least find *something*.

None of it works, though. You can't find ultimate satisfaction in any of those places or any others we try to find on our own. The Good Shepherd alone can lead us to green pastures and quiet waters.

John 4 tells of a woman who thought she was going to find satisfaction for her life on her own. Jesus finds her at a well in the heat of the day. She's been going from relationship to relationship, hoping to find the thing her soul longs for. The more she searches, the more she realizes she hasn't found it. So, she keeps chasing. She's had five husbands already at this point.

Having five husbands today gets people talking and gossiping. Relationship issues like that in those days were downright scandalous. Five husbands have come and gone, and now she is living with a man who isn't even her husband.

See a pattern here? She's chasing something and has never successfully grabbed hold of it. Most of us have been there at some point. Maybe not with relationships, but with something that we were sure would fill the need we had. It didn't.

Jesus meets that woman where she is, as she is. He doesn't throw her under the bus for being foolish or for making profound mistakes. Instead, He reminds her of this important truth: You will never quench your thirst drinking from empty wells. Only the living water can fill your soul. Stop chasing things that can never satisfy you. Drink from the Living Water, Jesus.

You've probably been trying to drink from empty wells. Whether it be relationships or substances, activities or busyness, you've gone to places thinking you'd find what you were looking for in them. But you didn't find true satisfaction, did you? Maybe you did for a moment, but it was only for a moment. It didn't last because it couldn't last. Your life was designed for something else.

The Good Shepherd loves you. He is leading you to a place where there will be green grass and quiet waters. The Shepherd is putting what will satisfy you right in front of you. He will satisfy your soul. Remember, we are never lacking. The Shepherd leads us to green pastures and ensures we lack no essential nourishment for our souls.

You have to choose to eat and drink. The Shepherd won't force you to. Don't be a stubborn sheep. Stop chasing what will always leave you empty and instead let the Bread of Life and Living Water fill you!

Questions for Today:

1. What well are you drinking from? Where is your go-to in your quest to find satisfaction and fulfillment?

2. If we know the Good Shepherd loves us and that He provides what we need so that we lack nothing, why do you think people resist resting in the green pastures and drinking from the quiet waters?

3. What is one way today that you can lie down in the green pastures?

Prayer for Today:

Lord, I often drink from wells that run dry. I fill my life with junk rather than with what nourishes. Help me today to find my contentment, fulfillment, and satisfaction in what You provide. Help me drink from what lasts and not from what is temporary.

Fill me up today as I graze in the green pastures and let me find refreshment in the quiet waters You have led me to.

Amen.

Week 2 Saturday and Sunday
I shall not want.
He makes me lie down in green pastures;
He leads me beside quiet waters.
Psalm 23:1–2

G o back and review the questions from this week's daily devotions.

1. In response to this week, how have you changed your view of what a *want* is?

2. What is one *want* you currently need to entrust to the Lord for Him to provide?

3. What is one area that this week's theme requires you to change?

4. Commit Psalm 23:1–2 to memory: "I shall not want. He makes me lie down in green pastures; He leads me beside quiet waters."

If you are able, go to church this week! Bless someone this weekend with a kind word or encouragement.

Week 3

He restores my soul;
He guides me in the paths of righteousness
For His name's sake.
Psalm 23:3

Week 3 Monday
He restores my soul.
Psalm 23:3

Some people have a hard time going to sleep. I am not one of them. I can count on one hand the number of sleepless nights I have encountered in my lifetime. Caffeine has no effect on me. I can drink energy drinks, cups of coffee, sodas, you name it, before bed, and as soon as I close my eyes, I am out.

I can sleep through storms, while riding in bumpy cars, and during loud movies. I have no trouble falling asleep.

Before you get too jealous, there is a catch. There is a reason for my ability to fall asleep quickly. And it isn't just a clean conscience. I may sleep easily, but that doesn't mean I rest well. Tonya will tell you I snore . . . loudly. I think she has been tempted to smother me in my sleep more than a few times. Not only do I snore, but I am told I hold my breath in my sleep. I can sleep soundly but then would wake up just as tired as when I went to bed. I was always tired. Elbows and closed fists weren't doing the trick. I needed some specialized help.

A visit to a sleep specialist revealed the issue. I have sleep apnea. Without help, I really do hold my breath in my sleep—sometimes up to a minute at a time, believe it or not. The result is I get plenty of sleep but no rest. I need help in the form of a CPAP machine that, when worn consistently, will make sure I breathe correctly and therefore rest well. The rest I can't find on my own comes easily when I lean on the right help.

When the text says, "He restores my soul," in verse 3, "restore" means to revive or reinvigorate. It is nothing less than a promise to give true rest to our souls. What a wonderful assurance!

The truth is, our souls need some reinvigoration. It is a lot harder for us to rest than we care to admit. It is easy for us to get worn out by all the pressures and expectations around us and within us. We are weary and worn.

Our tendency is to try a wide assortment of things in an attempt to refresh ourselves, but seldom are we able to engineer true rest. We will take vacations, self-medicate, or chase after things that will distract us from the constant pursuit of running on that hamster wheel. But, at the end of the day, and at the dawning of the next, we are just as weary as we were before. Here, then, is the problem. Even when we think we are resting, we never fully refresh. We need divine reinvigoration!

David is writing from personal experience. He understands what it means to be worn out. Throughout his life, as a shepherd, a warrior, and a king, he knows a thing or two about pouring it all out and needing a refreshing. God was faithful to always fill him up, just when he needed it. He says in Psalm 19 that the Word of the Lord restores his soul, and God's laws bring joy to his heart. As God speaks to him, and he anchors on those words, David finds his weary soul refreshed and his empty tank filled.

Do you need refreshment today? Are you feeling more than a little drained? Do you need some reinvigoration? Come to the Good Shepherd. He offers to fill your empty tank today.

Questions for Today:

1. What is your go-to for reinvigoration when you feel worn out?

2. How would you define true rest in your soul, and how can you find it?

3. David found refreshment in God's Word. What are some Bible verses that bring refreshment to you?

4. What does it require of you to move from self-made rest to true rest found in the Good Shepherd?

Prayer for Today:

Thank You, Lord, for restoring my soul when I am weary and worn out. You fill me up when I am empty. Help me rely on You and not seek ways on my own to fill that which only You can.
  Amen.

Week 3 Tuesday
He restores my soul.
Psalm 23:3

When your battery is empty, it matters how you seek to charge it.

My house gets broken into rather frequently. It is an unsolved mystery. I am surprised that by now they haven't turned this into a made-for-TV movie. I get robbed almost every week, it seems, and they have identified no suspects to this point. You see, every time I go to charge my phone, amazingly, I discover someone has stolen the charger.

Every. Single. Time.

To my knowledge, it is the only item ever taken. No one ever claims responsibility, and the authorities have not apprehended or charged any suspects. It is still an open investigation at this point.

I rely on my phone. Much of my life depends on it—banking information, social media accounts, calendar, photos. I'm not one who enjoys talking on the phone, but my cell phone is my primary means of communication with people. I'll text and email my family, friends, and coworkers all from that phone. When it goes dead, communication takes a significant hit. I need that phone charged. I need my charger. It is the only way my phone goes from dead to useful again. To make matters worse, for a long time, I needed a very particular charger. The charging port on my phone was corrupted, so I could only power up my phone with a wireless charger. I guarded that particular charger with my life. I knew that without it, my phone was as good as dead.

Knowing the phone is dead won't fix it. Being aggravated, angry, or sad about its condition doesn't change the reality of its condition. Knowing the means to power it back up isn't sufficient either. The only answer for a dead phone is to connect it to the correct source of power.

Our battery frequently runs low. We find ourselves in constant need of recharging. Unfortunately, most folks are unaware of how to restore their lives. They may be knowledgeable of the problem but can't seem to figure out how to plug in and get the refreshing they need.

Where does one go to get recharged? God's Word provides us with some excellent direction. In Psalm 19:7–8, King David says: "The law of the LORD is perfect, restoring the soul; The testimony of the LORD is sure, making wise the simple. The precepts of the LORD are right, rejoicing the heart; The commandment of the LORD is pure, enlightening the eyes."

There is something about spending time in the Word of God that refreshes the spirit. It restores the soul. The more you plug into the Word, the more recharged you are. It's like connecting a cell phone to a wall charger. David goes on later in Psalm 119:25, 37, 40, and 107 to proclaim that God's Word is the very thing that revives him. When your life's battery is drained, there is no substitute for spending time in the Bible. As you read, as you reflect, as you listen for His voice in the text, you find your spirit being uplifted.

If your cell phone battery is dead and you have a charger handy, it would be foolish not to connect the two together. The solution is right there. Unfortunately, we often find ourselves in a position where our spiritual battery is drained; we have easy access to the very thing that will energize us yet fail to put them together.

If your soul is feeling drained, plug into the Word of God. You'll notice a difference quickly. Try connecting to His Word today.

Questions for Today:

1. When you are feeling spiritually drained, what do you normally do to recharge?

2. How does God's Word provide refreshment to the soul?

3. What can you do today to establish a habit of spending time in God's Word more frequently?

Prayer for Today:

Thank You, Lord, for restoring my soul in those seasons when I feel empty. Your Word encourages and recharges me. Help me plug into the Scriptures as a daily habit. Help me make better use of the Bible You have made so readily available to me. Let me hunger and thirst for it because I know it revives a parched soul in a dry and weary land.

Amen.

Week 3 Wednesday
He restores my soul.
Psalm 23:3

New stuff never stays new. As soon as you buy it, it begins to wear out. It doesn't matter what the product is; wear and tear happens. That shiny new car is going to get some scratches and dents. That favorite sweater is going to get a hole in it. Shoes are going to get dirty, and the soles are going to wear out. It just happens. It is inevitable. You can take good care of things, and it may slow the process down, but you'll never stop it completely.

You may not be able to avoid wearing stuff out, but conversely, you sure can speed up the process. Take that new car and drive it off-road at 100 mph, and it is going to have an adverse effect on the car. Wear the sweater outside while you use the weed-eater to clean up your yard, and you'll discover it no longer looks store-quality. Wear those new shoes outside right after it has flooded, walk through some mud and grass, and the shine is gone for good.

Inevitably, our souls are going to need restoring and refreshing. It is a natural byproduct of living. Things in this world drain us, discourage us, and wear us out. It just happens. But there are some things that speed up the process of wearing us down. Sin is one of those things. Sin in our lives can quickly rob us of our joy and peace. It will weigh us down, burden us, and leave us weary and in desperate need of refreshment and restoration.

David is a man who understands this. There were seasons in his life when he needed renewal because of the difficulties of life, but there were also times he needed restoration because of poor decisions he had made. David was hanging out on the rooftop one day when he saw a pretty woman. He was, through his own doing, in the wrong place at the wrong time. David put himself in a terrible situation and then responded in a way that made it even worse. He decided he wanted that woman—who was married to someone else, as was David—to be his. So he used his power inappropriately and had her brought to him. What follows is a freefall of terrible choices—adultery, deception, murder. It is all bad.

His world started collapsing around him, and David's soul felt the weight of the wrong he had done. He carried around all that sin. It tore him up from the inside out. The weight of all that wrong pressed down on his soul and robbed him of God's joy. The more he allowed that sin to fester within him, the more downtrodden he was. However, the good news was David didn't stay there. Nathan the prophet confronted David about his sin, and as a result, he confessed that sin and turned from it. That confession began the process of refreshment and renewal for his soul.

David talks to the Lord about it and shares his words with us. We find it in Psalm 51:10–12:

Create in me a clean heart, O God, And renew a steadfast spirit within me. Do not cast me away from Your presence and do not take Your Holy Spirit from me. Restore to me the joy of Your salvation and sustain me with a willing spirit.

Renew. Restore. David understands. If he wants his soul to be restored and revived, it must begin with confession. You can't have a renewed soul and walk in willful disobedience. The sin must be confessed and turned from. Then renewal will come.

If you are weary and you need renewal of the soul, perhaps there is some sin in your life that you need to deal with first. Confess the sin and see what the Lord does as a result.

Questions for Today:

1. Is there sin in your life today that you've allowed to linger unconfessed longer than you should?

2. What areas of sin do you need to address and ask the Lord to forgive and restore to you the joy of your salvation?

3. In what one area of your life do you think something may be robbing you of your joy and, as a result,

wearying your soul?

Prayer for Today:

Lord, help me see those areas in my life that are displeasing to You. If there is sin I have allowed to take root in my life, please help me see it. Create in me a clean heart. Renew a steadfast spirit within me. Restore to me the joy of my salvation.

Amen.

Week 3 Thursday
He guides me in the paths of righteousness.
Psalm 23:3

We don't know what we are doing. Oh, we think we do, but we don't.

My boys loved LEGO sets when they were younger. My oldest was the personality type that followed the instructions to a T. He would pull the guidebook out and lay it alongside the box that had the finished product displayed on it. He would then follow each step just as instructed until the assembled contents looked exactly like the picture on the box. It may take hours or days, but he would construct the pieces just as directed, step by step. The end result was a creation that was just as it was designed to be.

Our life is like a box of LEGO toys. The only problem is the picture on the front of the box of what it should look like is missing, and the box contains approximately a billion tiny pieces that haven't been assembled yet.

The box is emptied onto the table in front of us, and we get to work. Each of us try our best to make something meaningful from the pieces we've been given. We work hard, putting each piece where we think it should go. Despite all our creativity and diligence, we end up making a mess of it all. We try to craft a masterpiece but end up with a monstrosity. It is a LEGO Frankenstein, figuratively speaking. The finished product may be supposed to look like the Mona Lisa, but our creation resembles nothing of the sort. It isn't a lack of effort. The reality is that we don't know what we are doing.

Thankfully, there is a Master Builder who knows not only exactly what the picture looks like but also knows how to assemble it so that it becomes what it is supposed to be. This Master is the one who designed it to begin with. He volunteers to help us take the pieces of our lives and put them together in the intended way. He is the only one who knows how to put it together. All we have to do is listen to His instructions.

The shepherd reveals his great care as he leads his sheep in directions that bring them blessing and not destruction. The sheep don't know where they are going or even where they should go. If left to wander, they will find themselves hungry, thirsty, lost, and easy prey for predators looking for a tasty snack. The sheep must rely on the shepherd to get them where they need to be. The shepherd knows the direction the sheep are to go.

With staff in hand, the shepherd leads the way. Across difficult terrain, over hills, through valleys, navigating field and forest. He doesn't need any counsel from the sheep; he knows the way. All the sheep need to do is watch the shepherd closely and follow where he is going.

Is it any wonder that the first words of Jesus to His disciples are, "Follow me"? Throughout His ministry, those words are His simple instructions to all who desire to be one of His people. He approaches Peter, Andrew, James, and John as they are in their boat and invites them to follow Him. Same thing for Matthew at the tax collecting booth. Same thing still when Jesus turns to the crowd and says, "If anyone wishes to come after Me, he must deny himself, and take up his cross and *follow Me*" (Mark 8:34, emphasis mine).

The call to every disciple from then until now has been the same. Follow Jesus. For over two thousand years, this has been the invitation and instruction. Jesus is that Good Shepherd who leads us, His sheep, to the paths of righteousness. Keep your eyes on Him and follow where He is going. He knows the direction and design for your life. Trust Him.

Take some time to listen for His voice and then follow where He leads.

Questions for Today:

1. How have you tried to build your life without looking at the instructions?

2. Sheep don't know where to go without the shepherd. How does the Good Shepherd give you direction?

3. What are the benefits of following Jesus as opposed to trying to figure out the path on your own?

4. Jesus's call is simply to follow. How can you follow that simple instruction today?

Prayer for Today:

Lord, help me have ears to hear Your voice as You call me to follow. Let me not rely on my own plans but set my feet on Your path. As a sheep listens to the shepherd's voice, help me listen only to the voice of my Good Shepherd.

Amen.

Week 3 Friday
He guides me in the paths of righteousness.
Psalm 23:3

I 'm thankful to live in a world that has the GPS (the Global Positioning System)! Long gone are the days of having to unfold maps or rely on an atlas. If you are looking to go somewhere and you don't know how to get there, simply type in the address and voilà, it instantly displays the directions. Right there on your phone, you can see the best route. It even provides alternative directions if the course needs to change because of an accident or road construction. The GPS calculates every turn and estimates approximate arrival times. Some GPS programs will even alert you to potential speed traps ahead (thanks for nothing, Rand McNally).

One of the best parts is the voice. You can choose from different voices to guide you through your GPS. Choices include different accents, from British to pirate. Yoda or Darth Vader can guide you. My personal favorite is Morgan Freeman. Who wouldn't want *that* voice guiding them? It sounds so trustworthy and reliable.

It may be those voices, but it is really still the GPS issuing the instructions. You don't have to look at your phone the whole time or at the display on the dashboard. There is a voice that guides you along the way. "In ten miles, turn left." "Stay in the center lane." "Slower traffic ahead."

Even with the GPS, I'll still miss turns. I will confuse a sudden right with a gradual turn and end up taking the wrong street. Even with the best directions, I can still go astray. It's in those moments I hear something like, "Make a U-turn ahead," or "Turn around!" Usually, I will have to hear those commands more than once. These are the reminders that tell me I am heading the wrong way until I correct my course.

GPS is so much better than just winging it. Imagine how much time I would waste if I were just trying to guesstimate how to get to where I want to go. I may never get there! I could miss it entirely. Or worse, I could end up in some place I didn't want or need to be.

I remember when I was a teenager, there was an area in town that was not the safest. In the middle of this area was an alley that was infamous among the local kids as being a dangerous place. It was a haven for dangerous folks, drug smugglers, kidnappers, and other seedy characters. In reality, it was probably more myth than truth—a cautionary tale of an area to be avoided at all costs. Whatever it was, it worked. As a new driver, trying to get from one part of town to the other, employing some "short cuts" that we just knew would get us to where we needed to be, some friends and I found ourselves headed down that alley one night. The panic crashed in upon us. Some scary-looking individuals began approaching the vehicle. As they surrounded the car, a knock on the window was followed by an ominous, "Roll down your window!" "What are you boys doing down here?"

Spinning tires could hardly get us out of there fast enough. I just remember thinking, "This is not where I am supposed to be!"

To get to where we are supposed to be on this road of life, this journey of faith, we need direction. We can't get to where we are supposed to be by winging it. Nor are we going to get there by guessing or taking short cuts we think will get us there. We need a spiritual GPS. Thankfully, we have one! And the voice is even more trusted than Morgan Freeman's!

John 10:27 says, "My sheep hear My voice, and I know them, and they follow Me." The Shepherd invites us to listen to His voice as He leads us to our destination. He is our guide, our navigation system. Through His Word, through His Spirit that lives within us, He directs our steps. Sometimes, we get off course. We hear His voice as He instructs us to turn around or make a U-turn ahead. Without listening to that voice, you will find yourself in places you didn't intend to be. Some, which are far away from God's direction for your life, will cause you to miss blessings He had for you. Others are places that bring hurt and harm. The Shepherd's trusted voice guides us down the path that leads to our blessing.

The Shepherd guides in the paths of righteousness. Follow His voice.

Questions for Today:

    1. What are some ways you can hear Jesus's voice guide

you in the direction He has for you?

2. When was a time listening to your own directions got you to a place you didn't want or need to be?

3. In a world where we have so many voices offering direction, how can you discern what His voice is from the competing voices around you?

Prayer for Today:

Lord, help me today to listen to Your voice as You lead me toward where You want me to be. Give me discernment as I tune out those voices that aren't Yours and keep me from the temptation of winging it on my own. Continue to lead me on the paths You have laid out for me.

Amen.

Week 3 Saturday and Sunday
He restores my soul; He guides me in the paths of righteousness for
His name's sake.
Psalm 23:3

G o back and review the questions from this week's daily devotions.

1. What is one specific way you will seek rest and renewal in the Lord this week?

2. How has this week's theme affected the way you will follow Jesus, the Shepherd?

3. What voices do you need to tune out so that you can clearly hear the Shepherd's voice guiding you?

4. Commit Psalm 23:3 to memory: "He restores my soul; He guides me in the paths of righteousness for His name's sake."

It's the weekend. What a great time to join other Christ-followers to worship the Lord! Send one thought from this week's devotions to a friend as an encouragement today.

Week 4

Even though I walk through the valley of the shadow of death, I fear no evil, for You are with me; Your rod and Your staff, they comfort me.
Psalm 23:4

Even though I walk through the valley of the shadow of death,
I fear no evil, for You are with me;
Your rod and Your staff, they comfort me.
Psalm 23:4

This verse in Psalm 23 provides a great transition in the text. In the previous verses, David writes about the Shepherd he knows so well. He relates truths about the God he serves and loves. As we have seen, he understands what it means to have a shepherd care for his sheep. He relays to the reader the truth that he has experienced by the Lord caring for him throughout his life.

Then, there is a shift. Beginning here, David no longer talks *about* the God he knows and instead starts talking *to* that One. Instead of saying "the Lord is," he moves to "You are." This subtle shift in tone reveals to us the nature of David's relationship to the Shepherd. David doesn't just know about the Lord. He knows the Lord personally. The psalm shifts from a discussion *about* the Good Shepherd to a conversation *with* the Good Shepherd. David isn't just giving us some facts about the Lord; he is inviting us into a prayer where he is speaking directly to the Lord Himself. It is an invitation to listen as he is speaking to *his* Shepherd.

It is one thing to know about someone and another thing entirely to know that individual personally. One of the people I am closest to is Matt. There are a lot of things I can share with you about him. I can tell you all you want to know about Matt and then some. I could tell you many details about Matt, from his childhood antics to his family and his career. After all, I know these things because I know him well; Matt's my dad. But hearing facts about him isn't the same as knowing him.

What if I let you be a participant in a conversation I was having with my dad? I can invite you to listen in on a call between my dad and me. Suddenly your understanding of who he is shifts. It moves you beyond information to relationship. You hear my dad's voice; you are privy to much more than facts and figures about who he is. You begin to see my dad through the prism of a personal conversation between two people who know and love each other.

David isn't just telling you about God; he is allowing you to lean in and meet Him through an intimate conversation with Him. David isn't talking about *a* shepherd; he is talking to *his* Shepherd. There is an intimacy in his words that reflects a deep personal relationship between himself, as a sheep, and the Lord as his Shepherd. These words David writes are not a cold discourse or lecture about a shepherd and his sheep. No, this is a beautiful conversation between two friends, two loved ones. It is personal and intimate.

Many people in our world know about God. They can list some facts and figures and tell some stories they know about Him. Far fewer actually know Him. They can say "He is" but would have a hard time sharing "You are."

The invitation in this passage is to know the Shepherd for yourself. To know more than that He cares for His sheep. To understand more than that He restores the souls of those who rest in Him. Not just to know He is guiding His sheep in the paths of righteousness. He wants you to know that He is guiding *you* in paths of righteousness—that He restores *your* soul. He wants you to know He cares for *you*. He wants *you* to know Him personally.

The question you have to ask is: Do you know about the Shepherd, or do you know the Shepherd?

Questions for Today:

1. If you were to describe the Lord today, how would you be able to describe Him? What is He to *you*?

2. Would you say you know more about the Lord or that you know the Lord through a relationship with Him?

3. What is the difference between knowing about the Lord and knowing the Lord?

Prayer for Today:

Lord, help me know You more each day. Don't let me be content with just knowing information about You. Let me know

You as my Shepherd, as my friend, as my deliverer. Help me, like David, to share my relationship with You with others so that they may know You too.

Amen.

Week 4 Tuesday
Even though I walk through the valley of the shadow of death,
I fear no evil, for You are with me;
Your rod and Your staff, they comfort me.
Psalm 23:4

S ome people like scary things; others do not. Whether it be
scary movies, haunted houses, or scary rides at amusement
parks, some folks like them and some don't. Some can't wait
to experience them; others can't get through them fast enough.
Often the determining factor is who is with them while they go
through it. Some of the biggest babies suddenly get brave if they
have the right fellow traveler. If they trust the one they are going
with, amazingly, they will tackle the fearful endeavor a little less
reluctantly.

Thunderstorms can be scary, especially big storms. There is
no doubt that a thunderstorm at night, when you are all alone,
can be frightening. Every bolt of lightning that crashes seems
to be right outside the window. The thunder rolling in sounds
dangerously close. The wind howling has you convinced that
the trees and limbs around you are all going to snap and fall in
on the house, crushing you. And if the lights go out . . . oh, the
terror!

However, if in that same storm, someone else is there with
you, the storm appears differently. If you are with friends, the
howling winds, lightning, and thunder are not quite as terrifying. You might even laugh during it. If you are a child and your

parents are close by, you can sleep while the thunder crashes. You find peace in the presence of those you trust and love, even as the storm rages.

It is important to see that the text here says "walk through the valley of the shadow of death" not "run through the valley of the shadow of death." You run through fearful things; you walk when there is peace. When we face frightening things, it is good to know the Lord is always with us. He is the source of comfort and strength, regardless of what we are facing. We can walk peacefully through any situation, death included, if we know He is with us. We aren't running scared; we are walking boldly with the Lord leading us.

Joshua took over for Moses and was to lead God's people into the promised land. It was a land of milk and honey but also a land filled with armies, fortified cities, giants, and plenty of unknowns. Potential death loomed on the horizon. But God gave Joshua a word before he ever stepped foot into the promised land. He said multiple times to Joshua first and then the people, "Be strong and courageous!" He also gave a reason they shouldn't be afraid: "For the Lord your God is with you wherever you go" (Joshua 1:9). They were going into the unknown, but they were traveling led by One they knew. One who would never leave them. One who would provide everything they needed along the way. As long as He was there, they didn't need to be afraid of anything.

That same God is with us today. He promises to remain present with us throughout all our lives, even when we walk through the valley of the shadow of death. We don't have to be afraid, for He is with us. Paul will say nothing "will be able to separate us from the love of God, which is in Christ Jesus our Lord" (Romans 8:39). In other words, the world can't throw anything at us that would separate Christ from us. He is with us even in the most fearful moments. Even while we are walking through the valley of the shadow of death.

Is there something that has you anxious right now? Remember His presence with you even in uncertain and frightening times.

Questions for Today:

1. What situations are you afraid of today?

2. How can you know Jesus will never abandon you in a time of need?

3. If Jesus is with you on this road of faith, what is there for you to be fearful of?

Prayer for Today:

Thank You, Lord, for always being with me. Thank You for walking with me through the valleys and storms that come my way. Help me remember when I am afraid, that You are with me and will never leave me. Help me walk with boldness no matter what I face.

Amen.

Week 4 Wednesday

Even though I walk through the valley of the shadow of death,
I fear no evil, for You are with me;
Your rod and Your staff, they comfort me.
Psalm 23:4

It's one thing to say we'll never lack for anything; it's another thing entirely to believe that is true. We envision all kinds of scenarios where we discover a great need and then realize we don't have enough to survive. The what-ifs are endless:

What if there is a pile of bills to pay and your bank account is hitting on zero?

What if there are deadlines looming and time is quickly running out?

What if you've got to get to work and your car decides to quit on you?

What if you have to make a good grade on a test to pass the course and you still don't understand the material?

What if, what if, what if.

We've all been there. We are keenly aware of a need and then look around only to realize that the provisions we need aren't materializing. The anxiety level goes up, and if we aren't careful, our faith level goes down. When we can't see how the Shepherd is going to provide, we take matters into our own hands to provide for ourselves. In doing so, we often miss the blessing that He was about to provide if we would have only trusted that He had it under control.

It is important to realize that the Shepherd sees things differently from the sheep. He has a better view. He knows not only the needs of His sheep, but how best to meet those needs. In fact, sometimes the needs the sheep are sure they have are not really the needs they have at all. There may be a more pressing need that the Shepherd must address. Maybe the need really isn't about a bank account that is depleted. Maybe the need isn't about the time or resources you don't have. Maybe there is a bigger need that you can't yet see. While all you may see is the immediate, the Shepherd is providing for something far greater.

In Mark 4, we find a great story of some guys who are absolutely sure of a need they have that isn't being met. You've got Jesus and the twelve disciples in a boat, heading across the Sea of Galilee. Suddenly, a fierce storm kicks up, throwing the boat and its passengers around in a violent upheaval. The wind is howling; the waves are crashing hard, and the boat is filling up with water. The disciples see the situation. They are going under. They are going to die. What greater need could there possibly be?

Jesus is with them. He is undisturbed by the storm. Now I can sleep through almost anything, but here Jesus is fast asleep in what seems to be the most frightening storm these guys have ever seen. The men wake Jesus and fuss at Him.

"Don't you care we are about to die!?" they said.

Jesus gets up and does two things. First, He rebukes the storm and tells it to be quiet. It stops its fury in an instant.

Then, He turns His attention to the disciples.

He doesn't tell them, "Glad you woke me so I could handle your need."

Nope. He fusses at them.

He says, "Why are you afraid? Where is your faith?"

It is easy to be afraid, especially in the presence of death. For most of us, death seems to be the very thing that elicits the most fear. If the shadow of death tempts you to be fearful, you are in good company. Throughout Scripture, the Lord speaks to those who find themselves afraid as potential death is on the horizon.

I think of the disciples in that boat in the middle of the ferocious storm. The violent sea has them distracted and disrupted. They were facing what they believed was imminent death and were afraid. They weren't sure Jesus even cared about what would happen to them. Yet, with a word, Jesus silences the wind and waves and their hearts too. "Peace, be still." In that valley of the shadow of death, Jesus brought peace.

It was to be their last evening together, though they didn't know it. Jesus knew that in a matter of a few hours, the religious leaders would arrest Him and haul Him away. Worse, He knew of the coming beatings, abuse, and crucifixion. His death was only a matter of hours away. Faced with what would happen to Him, Jesus speaks words of assurance to the disciples. "Do not let your heart be troubled" (John 14:1). Death was on the horizon, but Jesus didn't want them to be afraid or undone. He tells them, "Peace I leave with you; My peace I give to you" (John 14:27). Their world was about to be wrecked. They were about to have the very thing, the very One, who was their rock, crushed before them. And yet Jesus didn't want His friends to come undone. Though in the middle of a terrible storm, Jesus was still saying, "Peace, be still."

They saw a need. Jesus wanted them to see *Him* and know that they didn't have to worry about the need. He's got it.

How is that kind of peace even possible? Paul issues this challenge in Philippians 4:4-7:

> Rejoice in the Lord always; again I will say, rejoice! Let your gentle spirit be known to all men. The Lord is near. Be anxious for nothing, but in everything by prayer and supplication with thanksgiving let your requests be made known to God. And the peace of God, which surpasses all comprehension, will guard your hearts and minds in Christ Jesus.

Peace is possible because Jesus is near. The Good Shepherd is ever present, even in the valley of death.

In the storm, Jesus is present. When it looks like things are in chaos and tumult, Jesus is still in control. Jesus is in control in the boat, in the upper room, in Pilot's court, on the cross, and in the tomb. Things may have been uncertain to the disciples, but there was never a doubt as to the outcome for Jesus. They simply had to trust Him. That trust during the storm produced peace. The winds may blow, but Jesus has them.

David may walk through what appears to be a valley of the shadow of death, but God still has him. He doesn't have to be afraid as long as he remembers the Shepherd is always near.

The Shepherd is with us. Jesus knows our situations far better than we do. It may be true that the needs are significant around us. All we may feel are the wind and waves of the storm. Our boat may seem to fill up. That can be a scary proposition. However, Jesus is still in the boat with us. He will not let us drown. Our greatest need in that moment is not that He calm the storm, but that we trust Him amid the storm. As long as the Shepherd is with us, the sheep just need to trust that He will provide what we need as we need it.

Let this encourage you today! The Shepherd is with us, even in the valley of the shadow of death.

Questions for Today:

1. In times of struggle, do you find it hard to trust the Shepherd to provide for the needs you have?

2. In what ways do you sometimes try to take over and meet needs yourself?

3. How does it feel when you see the Shepherd provide in ways you didn't expect?

4. What is one example of a need you had that was provided for by Jesus alone?

Prayer for Today:

Lord, I trust You to meet the needs I have. Trusting You doesn't mean I walk recklessly. You call me to walk wisely. I am choosing to rely on You to provide what I need today. You see things clearer than I do; You have better resources than I do, and You have the plan for my life that brings blessing. As my Shepherd, take care of me, Your sheep, today.

Amen.

Even though I walk through the valley of the shadow of death,
I fear no evil, for You are with me;
Your rod and Your staff, they comfort me.
Psalm 23:4

T he path may not always be easy. It may not always be smooth. The way may be challenging, filled with obstacles to navigate. Sometimes, the journey will leave you bruised. But the road is always worth it.

Solomon, the wisest man to ever live, says in Proverbs 3:5–6, "Trust in the Lord with all your heart and do not lean on your own understanding. In all your ways acknowledge Him, and He will make your paths straight."

Straight. Not easy.

Straight. Not pain free.

Straight. Not smooth.

The point is, if you will trust Him and follow Him rather than going in the directions you think are right, the Lord will get you where you need to be.

I have two sisters, both older than I am. When I was in junior high, one of them was dating a guy who, as you would expect, was at our house frequently. I was just a goofy kid, and it would have been completely understandable for him to completely ignore my existence. After all, I was just the kid brother of a then-current love interest. But for whatever reason, he treated me differently. He was kind and gracious to me. On one occasion, when he was at the house, he invited me and some of my junior high buddies on a journey. An adventure. He knew the area we lived in, having lived in the general area a lot longer than we had. Out the back door we went; where we were going, we did not know. We were simply following him wherever the adventure led. Across a field into some densely packed woods, we trekked. I had explored those woods before but had never gone quite this same way. Under some thick brush, through some thickets and briers. Through a mostly dried-up creek bed.

It seemed we had been traveling forever, and then suddenly we were there. An opening in the woods revealed a junior high kid's paradise. Emerging into a clearing, we discovered an old, abandoned log cabin. An adventurers delight! We spent the rest of our day climbing and exploring that site. It was incredible. We discovered it, but he always knew it was there. We never would have found it except that he was willing to lead us there. He knew where it was and how to get there. We simply had to follow him. He could have just told us it existed, but instead, he showed us and let us experience it firsthand.

It wasn't easy to get to. I got scratched up in the process. But the briers were worth the blessing.

There is a road God has for you to travel. It leads to blessing and life. He could have just told us that the road existed, that the blessing was somewhere out there, but instead, He leads us there Himself. The Lord is our personal guide on the journey. He knows every step to take, every turn to make. He alone can get us to where He created us to go. As we navigate, it will be a challenge. There will be bumps and bruises along the way. Scratches and scrapes. There may even be times when you are ready to quit and just head back to the comfort of home. But believe me, it is all worth it. Every single step. You can't get to the blessing without traveling through some briers. Keep your eyes on Jesus and let Him take you on an incredible adventure.

Sometimes to get to the blessed green pastures, you've got to travel through the dark valleys. It is worth the journey.

Questions for Today:

1. What adventure have you experienced that required an investment in blood, sweat, and tears?

2. What provides inspiration for you to keep moving forward down the road He has for you, even when the path is difficult?

3. What blessing have you received from the Lord by following Him down rocky paths?

4. In what direction do you see God leading you that may require you stepping out of your comfort zone?

Prayer for Today:

Lord, give me the strength to travel the tough roads and hard paths that You lead me down. I know Your way is best and leads to blessing for me, Your sheep. Deepen my faith and trust in You as I follow close to You.

Amen.

Week 4 Friday
Even though I walk through the valley of the shadow of death,
I fear no evil, for You are with me;
Your rod and Your staff, they comfort me.
Psalm 23:4

A s much as we hate to think about it, death is an ever-present reality. People die. People we know. People we love. People like us.

We live with the expectation that death looms just out in front of us. The older we get, the greater the understanding. All of us, one day, will taste death. Some days, death seems a lot closer than others.

We live seconds from death at any time. When I was in college, I grabbed a bite to eat at a local fast-food restaurant. I saw on the news later that evening that there had been a shooting, with someone being killed, in that same place just moments after I left. Close call. My father-in-law was driving around in his truck with his pastor during a storm, and a tree suddenly fell and crushed the car. They escaped death, but it sure was close. Near misses. We've all been there, just moments from disaster, missing a certain demise by inches or seconds. All of us are walking through the valley of the shadow of death David talks about.

Sheep live in that same kind of world. A robber or wolf is lurking around every corner. However, the sheep need not live in fear. There is a shepherd to protect them. They need not concern themselves with the prospect of what is around the corner as long as that shepherd is walking with them. The shepherd had his rod and staff, tools of comfort and care. The rod was a weapon to protect against those who would seek to harm his sheep. A staff was a tool of rescue. With its crook, the shepherd could gently pull his sheep from dangerous paths and places. These tools in and of themselves were powerless, but in the shepherd's hands, powerful instruments of care and comfort.

It is quite possible for you and me to live in constant fear of the reality of death. We could let the reality of the closeness of death be an overbearing force that weighs us down, preventing us from moving forward. However, as long as the Good Shepherd is leading us as we walk through that deathly shadow, we need not be concerned with what might be. He still protects us from that which threatens around us. He gently pulls us from dangerous paths that would harm us.

As true as the reality of death is, the reality of the protecting Shepherd is even truer. The promise of Scripture is that even when death casts its pale shadow upon us, and we pass through not only the *valley* of death, but through its *very doors,* we do not have to be afraid. The Good Shepherd has His sheep in that moment too.

Jesus, as He was preparing His disciples for His own death, said this:

Do not let your heart be troubled; believe in God, believe also in Me. In My Father's house are many dwelling places; if it were not so, I would have told you; for I go to prepare a place for you. If I go and prepare a place for you, I will come again and receive you to Myself, that where I am, there you may be also. And you know the way where I am going." Thomas said to Him, "Lord, we do not know where You are going, how do we know the way?" Jesus said to him, "I am the way, and the truth, and the life; no one comes to the Father but through Me." (John 14:1–6)

The Good Shepherd, Jesus, tells His closest friends, in a moment that would lead them through a valley filled with dark shadows, that they shouldn't let their hearts come undone. They are to trust Him, even when everything in them says to be afraid. He was preparing a place for them on the other side of the valley. It may be dark for a moment, but He was leading His sheep to a place just on the other side that was something beautiful. All they had to do was trust Him. The valley wasn't the final destination—just a passing scene on their way to new green pastures and quiet waters.

Times might seem dark for you. The certainty of life is that people you love will pass through that valley of the shadow of death. It may seem to engulf them and leave you fearful.

The truth is, eventually you'll approach that valley too. It will seem frightening and could cause you to be shaken. When that happens, just keep trusting your Shepherd. He will be with you.

I've got good news for you. Whatever you are going through, the Good Shepherd will walk with you. He will get you to the other side. Trust Him.

Questions for Today:

1. What was a "close call" that you experienced that reminded you how fragile life is? How did that make you feel?

2. How can you find peace even when you or someone you love is walking through that shadow of death?

3. In what way does knowing "the way, the truth, and the life" affect how you walk through that valley?

4. If the valley of the shadow of death is just a scene to pass through on the way to green pastures, how can that shape the way you view the death of someone who knows the Good Shepherd?

Prayer for Today:

Lord, help me keep my eyes fixed on the Shepherd when I walk through seasons of death and loss. Comfort me and strengthen me as You lead me through that dark valley to the green pastures and quiet waters ahead.

Amen.

Week 4 Saturday and Sunday
Even though I walk through the valley of the shadow of death,
I fear no evil, for You are with me;
Your rod and Your staff, they comfort me.
Psalm 23:4

G o back and review the questions from this week's daily devotions.

1. How has this week's theme of God's presence in times of fear changed your perspective?

2. What is one fear you will entrust to the Shepherd this week?

3. In times of fear, do you run ahead, freeze, or walk with the Shepherd? What evidence supports this opinion?

4. Commit Psalm 23:4 to memory: "Even though I walk through the valley of the shadow of death, I fear no evil, for You are with me; Your rod and Your staff, they comfort me."

Make your plan now to attend a gathering with other believers this weekend. Experience the blessing of worshipping together.

Week 5

*You prepare a table before me in the presence of my enemies; You
have anointed my head with oil; my cup overflows.*
Psalm 23:5

You prepare a table before me in the presence of my enemies;
You have anointed my head with oil;
my cup overflows.
Psalm 23:5

I may not have the best choices in the teams I pull for, but if nothing else, I am a dedicated fan. Win or lose, I get personally invested in my team's every sporting event. I have traveled to watch more than my fair share of football, baseball, and basketball games. Not all of them end in triumph. In fact, many end in agonizing defeat. Some are lopsided victories; some are blowout losses. The most stressful ones are those that seem to hang in the balance until the last moment. Bottom of the ninth, two outs, bases loaded, down by a run. Late fourth quarter and my team has the ball trailing by a field goal. With just a few seconds on the clock and down by a basket, my team gets possession of the ball. Those games will wreck you!

As I have gotten older and moved farther away from the teams I love, I've attended fewer games than I did earlier in life. My passion for the team hasn't waned, but my ability to see them in person has become limited. However, thanks to modern technology, though I may not be there, I can still watch the games live on demand. I can be hundreds, even thousands of miles away, and still enjoy the game in real time. Better yet, it's available for viewing on my own schedule. Game at 11 a.m.? I can watch it at my convenience at 6 p.m. I will see the same thing that those in the stadium saw, just at a different time. What happens will always remain the same no matter when I actually see it unfold.

There have been some games I have watched that, as I watched them, the outcome seemed grim. November 11, 2021, was such a time. The Mississippi State Bulldogs, my team since birth, were playing on the road against the ranked Auburn Tigers. I wasn't at the game and couldn't watch it live, so I recorded it to watch when I got home. As I watched it, I was ready to turn it off by halftime. The game started horribly! The Bulldogs were down 28-3 in the first half. It just wasn't the Dawgs' day, apparently. However, what I didn't know was that though the score I saw was 28-3, that was not the final score. My team scored forty unanswered points on the way to a 43-34 victory! That was the present reality, as I was watching it, even though what I was witnessing didn't reveal it yet.

What I saw on the screen wasn't an accurate reflection of what had already happened. Though it appeared to be a dire situation, the game had already ended in victory. How foolish it was to fret and worry when that was not an accurate picture of how things were!

Here in Psalm 23, David's enemies are around him. Hemmed in, the situation seems serious. However, we don't find David anxious or afraid. Stress hasn't chased away his appetite, and his stomach isn't bound up in knots. Instead, he is sitting comfortably at a dinner table prepared for him. Reclining at the table, David is enjoying a peaceful meal. It wasn't in the absence of the surrounding threat, but rather in the middle of it. How is that possible? David understands that what he sees around him is not a true representation of what is happening. God has already taken care of the matter at hand. Just because David hasn't seen the ultimate result yet doesn't change the reality that, in real time, God has it under control and the victory assured.

Throughout Scripture, God assures His people that regardless of what their eyes may tell them, they should take courage; He has the victory won. When Joshua enters the promised land, which, as of their last scouting report, was filled with fortified cities and giant warriors, God assures him that all is over but the shouting.

David experienced the same reality earlier in his life. The odds were stacked heavily in Goliath's favor. A nine-feet-tall trained killer with armor and a massive sword versus a boy shepherd with a slingshot. Anyone with eyes would tell you this was going to be a bloodbath . . . in favor of the giant. But God knows the score, and it isn't David against Goliath. It is God versus Goliath, and the giant is no match for God Almighty.

Joshua, David, and countless others of God's people move with confidence because they understand that the Lord's presence with them is enough to give them peace and rest even as adversaries circle around them. The enemy may be boisterous, but they just haven't seen the final score yet.

Paul says it this way in Romans 8:35–39:

Who will separate us from the love of Christ? Will tribulation, or distress, or persecution, or famine, or nakedness, or peril, or sword? Just as it is written, "For Your sake we are being put to death all day long; We were considered as sheep to be slaughtered." But in all these things we overwhelmingly conquer through Him who loved us. For I am convinced that neither death, nor life, nor angels, nor principalities, nor things present, nor things to come, nor powers, nor height, nor depth, nor any other created thing will be able to separate us from the love of God, which is in Christ Jesus our Lord.

There are all kinds of situations that, at first glance, may appear to say to us, "You are not winning here. You are in big trouble." Distress, persecution, peril, and so on don't seem too much like winning. However, Paul is clear. The things you currently see don't reflect the reality of what truly is. Even in all that mess, Paul says we are more than conquerors!

Our enemies come in all different forms. For some, there are real people who stand in opposition to us. Individuals may try to cause us harm. We find them in our workplaces, social spaces, and so many other contexts. For others, the enemy may be situations that actively work against us. Financial struggles, health concerns, personal conflicts, addictions and destructive habits. Enemies may go by different names, but we know them well. Some seasons feel like we are overwhelmed and surrounded by them.

It's easy to see the enemy's presence around you and be fearful. We often rely on what we presently see and not on what is already assured. Sometimes it looks like we are in danger of defeat, even if the final score tells us something different. It might not be an army or a giant, but it isn't hard to identify the enemies that seem to close in around us. Struggle and trials, closed doors and missed opportunities, fear and failure, persecution and opposition all seem to scream, "This is not winning!" Check the final box score. You're only seeing the first quarter. It isn't over yet. You win in the end because of Christ.

Questions for Today:

1. What "enemy" tempts you to forget the victory you have been assured in Christ?

2. How can knowing the final score impact how you walk through difficulty today?

3. How is David able to eat peacefully even with enemies around him?

4. What does eating peaceably at the table mean for you?

Prayer for Today:

Lord, help me today to understand that even though it may seem like I'm surrounded by struggles and difficulty, I only see part of the picture. Help me continue to rest at Your table, assured by the victory You have already won. Let me live a life that reflects victory and not defeat.

Amen.

Week 5 Tuesday
You prepare a table before me in the presence of my enemies;
You have anointed my head with oil;
my cup overflows.
Psalm 23:5

In tough times, help can sometimes be hard to find. I witnessed this firsthand in the days after Hurricane Katrina. The storm hit my little out-of-the-way Louisiana town hard. Some folks left town before the storm hit. Others like me chose to ride it out. When the hurricane rolled through, it brought with it an intense fury. Trees snapped like toothpicks, wind blew away awnings, roofs, and whatever stood in its path. By the time it was done, the town had lost power, and Katrina had left debris scattered everywhere, homes destroyed and lives upended. It looked like a war zone.

The days that followed were difficult. In the scorching August sun, there was no air conditioning to be found. Water was in short supply. Armed guards had to patrol the local gas stations as limited fuel was available. The people needed relief, and that relief was scarce. Our town seemed to be forgotten, cut off from the rest of the world. Because of our remote location, state officials even had difficulty sending help.

However, in the days that followed, something amazing happened. Help arrived from an unlikely source. Not unlikely because it was out of character for them to help. Unlikely because they were coming to a place like ours to help. We weren't a big city, a strategic area, or a place with any advantage for them. Yet, they came into our struggle and brought the resources and relief we needed. Early one morning, in rolled the Southern Baptist Disaster Relief crews. The feeding unit and chainsaw teams showed up and showed out for the next several weeks, meeting our physical needs and bringing with them encouragement to a ravaged town.

David says the Lord prepares a table in the presence of his enemies. In the presence of, not in the absence of. God's care isn't dependent on things going well. Nothing limits His care to times when the enemy isn't around. God moves right past the mess and the threat and sets a table of provision for David to enjoy. God isn't concerned about the enemy being around. David doesn't have to fret about what is going on around him. God assures David of His care for him even in the most threatening moments. He doesn't have to stand at the door and watch the enemies' movements. David doesn't have to labor to fortify his position to ensure his own safety. He simply has to sit down, rest, and eat. All of this is done with the peace of mind that God sets the table, gives him what he needs, and he is to enjoy the provision.

Psalm 46:1–3 gives this assurance:

> God is our refuge and strength, A very present help in trouble. Therefore we will not fear, though the earth should change and though the

mountains slip into the heart of the sea; Though
its waters roar and foam, Though the mountains
quake at its swelling pride.

There is a temptation to stress in the storm, to worry if God
will come through when things are tough. David can testify
what the writer of Psalm 46 says. When you find yourself in
the tumult, God is a place of security. He is the refuge for us
to hide in, the strength when our own strength falters. The last
words of the psalm say that we are to be still and know that He
is God. Other translations read something like, cease striving
and remember who God is. In other words, stop fretting and
coming apart at the seams. Sit down at the table and eat. God
has got this.

When trouble arises, God doesn't run away; He comes
through. When your life gets turned upside down, He doesn't
skip out of town. He moves in and provides just what you need.
Pull up a chair and enjoy your meal. He has got you.

Questions for Today:

1. What does it mean to you that God prepares a table
for you in the presence of your enemies, not after the
enemies are gone?

2. How have you seen God respond to you in the middle

of a hardship?

3. Is it hard for you to rest at the table when you see enemies around? Why or why not?

4. What does it mean for you to "be still" and sit and eat at the table He has provided for you?

Prayer for Today:

Thank You, Lord, for not abandoning me when conflict came. Thank You for showing up to prepare a place of peace and rest, even as the storms rage around me. Help me continue to find rest and peace in You, regardless of what is going on around me.

Amen.

Week 5 Wednesday

You prepare a table before me in the presence of my enemies;
You have anointed my head with oil;
my cup overflows.
Psalm 23:5

P salm 4:8 says, "In peace I will both lie down and sleep, For
You alone, O LORD, make me to dwell in safety."

It is easy to lose your appetite in times of trouble. When
faced with a conflict or difficulty, your stomach tends to get
all tied up in knots. Butterflies fill the belly, and the last thing
you want to do is eat. Years ago, while I was a young student
minister, I had an issue with the interim pastor who was leading
my church. Or rather, he had an issue with me. The staff at the
church, including myself, complained about a decision he was
making; we had some ethical concerns. When we approached
him about the matter, he saw it as a personal attack. Rather than
talk through it, he went scorched earth on all those who spoke
up, including this unsuspecting young minister. He made many
threats and promises about my remaining days in ministry, and
he assured me he was going to make sure there would not be
many left.

I knew I had done nothing wrong, but the threats he made
rocked my world. The situation undid me. Dread overtook me
because I was certain about the coming onslaught that would
surely end my ministry. It consumed my thoughts, and I felt sick
to my stomach. I could just throw up. Panic and distress washed

over me. I had a family to provide for, and I was just a relatively inexperienced minister pitted against a seasoned pastor. The odds were against me. What could I do?

Then the Lord reminded me of an important truth. The Shepherd doesn't abandon His sheep when the wolves attack!

In a way that only God could do, He provided. He placed others in the church to serve as advocates for me even when I could not advocate for myself. The Lord provided people to stand in the gap and watch out for me. The church didn't fire me, and many years of ministry there followed. God saved the day once again.

What a picture David paints for us in verse 5! The enemy is encamping all around him, pushing in on him from all sides. They are plotting. They are planning. An attack could come at any moment. The enemy's goal is David's defeat. They hoped that their very presence would strike terror into the heart of David. As they spied out the situation, they fully expected to see David in full reactionary mode. Rally the troops, make the plans, prepare for war. They expected to see a king stressed out and in a frantic rush. There would be no rest for him tonight!

They look in, and what do they see? David is reclining at the table enjoying a banquet feast prepared just for him. There is no panic. No chaos or confusion. Just peace. The peace isn't present because of the absence of an enemy attack. It is peace despite the enemy's attacks. David, fully aware of the circling enemy, has a full belly and a peace-filled heart knowing God is in control. It isn't his battle to fight; it is the Lord's. And he knew the Lord could handle it. So there David sits in the presence of the attackers, and instead of fretting, he is feasting. And all the enemy could do was watch. Whether they knew it or not, the enemy was already defeated.

Remember, even when things look dark, the battle is already over. Because of the Good Shepherd leading us, we win in the end! Rest well.

Questions for Today:

1. When has fear, conflict, or anxiety robbed you of your "appetite" for peace?

2. How might God be inviting you to sit at His table instead of letting worry consume you?

3. David rested at the banquet table even with enemies surrounding him. What would it look like in your current situation to trust God enough to feast instead of fret?

4. Think about a time when someone opposed, criticized, or misunderstood you. How did you respond, and how might you respond differently today if you truly believed the battle belongs to the Lord?

5. Psalm 4:8 reminds us that God alone makes us "dwell in safety." Where in your life do you need to stop striv-

ing to defend yourself and instead rest in the peace of God's protection?

Prayer for Today:

Lord, help me rest today, knowing that even if my enemy camps around me, You are still fighting the battle. Help me see Your provision of peace and allow me to feast on that which You have blessed me with even amid conflict.

Amen.

Week 5 Thursday
You prepare a table before me in the presence of my enemies;
You have anointed my head with oil;
my cup overflows.
Psalm 23:5

P art of not being in want, having that table prepared, and having our cup overflow means that we always have exactly what we need to do what God calls us to do. That is an important thing to remember because there will be seasons where you don't feel like that is the case. You will know God is calling you to something, but when you look at what you have, you quickly discover that you don't have enough to do it. The table will seem bare and the cup empty. However, your estimation of what you have and what you need may differ significantly from what God sees.

David is facing a giant.

Not a figurative one, but a real one.

Snarling, menacing, and powerful. He has the entire army of Israel quaking in their sandals. Well-armed soldiers are unwilling to go toe to toe with this warrior.

Then up walks this kid with nothing. He has no military training, no mighty shield or sword. He is just a shepherd. It is laughable. The king offers him his armor, but the kid won't take it. He knows what he has to do and walks out onto the battlefield to face a monster of a man.

We can't turn away from a train wreck, but I bet Israel's soldiers don't want to watch what was about to happen.

It is certain to be a slaughter.

On the one side there is a killer, a champion warrior heads and shoulders above everyone else. He is well-trained and well-equipped for battle. He has the armor, the sword, a javelin, and a shield bearer ahead of him.

On the other side is this boy. A shepherd with nothing. It is a mismatch. The boy doesn't have enough to fight, much less win. All he has in his arsenal is a sling and some stones. Paper may beat rock, rock beats scissors, and scissors beat paper, but in wartime, sword and shield beat sling and stone every single time.

First Samuel 17 tells how the story unfolds. We may have gotten familiar with the story, but imagine hearing it for the first time. An unarmed, or at least inadequately armed, boy versus a well-trained giant assassin. This should not end well for the boy. He lacks what he needs to even be in the fight.

But what do you know? A real David versus Goliath story!

Sling and stone *do* beat shield and sword. David has exactly what he needs to face the giant. It may not seem like much; by anyone else's standards it may not be adequate for the fight, but it is enough. David lacks for nothing.

Now you know that isn't the only story we find in the Bible about God's people having exactly what they need to accomplish what He calls them to do. After all, didn't some disciples feed well over five thousand people with nothing more than a glorified Happy Meal? Five loaves and two fish don't appear to be enough to satisfy the growling stomachs of all those hangry people—so hungry they are angry. But they want for nothing—lack for nothing. The table is full; the cup overflows. They have exactly what they need, even if from the outside world it looks like it isn't enough.

I don't know what you are facing today. I don't know what it is God is calling you to do. It may be to face some Goliath. He may call you to feed a multitude. It could be a great opportunity or a perceived challenge. The temptation may arise in you to look at whatever is ahead of you and think you can't face it because you don't have what you need. You may feel you need an army and all you have is a sling and stones. You may think you need an all-you-can-eat buffet, but all you have is a snack pack. The Shepherd is leading you. You have everything you need. If He is leading you to it, He will provide what you need to get through it. It doesn't matter what you bring to the table; trust your Shepherd. You may not have enough, but He always does.

Today, if you feel like everything is stacked against you, remember that with God on your side, He gives you everything you need!

Questions for Today:

1. What are some challenges you are facing right now?

2. Do you feel you have enough to face these challenges?

3. If you were David, how would you have felt walking out to face that giant with only a sling in your hand?

4. How have you seen God use what you had to meet needs that seemed so great?

Prayer for Today:

Lord, help me remember giants can fall with slings and stones when we trust You. Today, let me see the resources You've entrusted to me not through my own eyes, but through Yours. I have exactly what I need to face whatever You lead me toward. Let me rely on both Your direction and Your provision.

Amen.

Week 5 Friday
My cup overflows.
Psalm 23:5

M ost people live with their tanks almost empty. We run wide open all the time—full throttle. We are running here, there, and everywhere. The problem is not that some stuff is good, and some is bad. No, it's just that we continually run. We're chasing life full time. We are running after school or work. Chasing family activities. Headed to church. Involved in social activities. We have a never-ending list of places to be, things to do, and people to see. In all that running, we take little or no time to refuel the tank.

If the promise in Psalm 23 is a cup that overflows, why do so many people feel like their plate is overflowing but their cup is empty?

You can't run wide open forever. Eventually, you run out of gas or the batteries die. Leave a flashlight on 24/7, and you'll find it growing progressively dimmer and then completely off. The same is true for you and me. A life constantly on the go is sure to run out of gas eventually.

We never seem to run out of gas at opportune times. It is usually at the most inconvenient moments or unhelpful places. One evening, I was hanging out with my roommates in my college apartment. For reasons I don't remember, two of us decided we'd head to my house to pick up something long since forgotten. It wasn't a crazy idea. My house was barely half an hour away. I had a little two-seat Honda, so two of us jumped in and hit the road.

I noticed right away that I was low on gas, but there was no need for alarm since (A) my house wasn't that far away, (B) the car got like a million miles a gallon, and (C) the gas light hadn't come on.

Off we went. We were about a mile from the city limits of my town when we made an important discovery.

The Honda had no gas light.

As we sputtered to a stop, it painfully reminded me that without gas in the tank, you aren't getting very far. What followed was a miserable evening of pushing the car to the nearest gas station.

The gas gauge said empty, but I was sure I still had enough. I kept waiting for the light to come on until it was too late.

Sheep need fuel in their tanks too. They're not the Energizer Bunny. The shepherd's job is to make sure the sheep get the nourishment and refreshment they need. That is what David was talking about in verses 2 and 5. The two places where a sheep can fill its tank are green pastures and quiet waters. And when they rest in those places, they find their cup overflows. The good shepherd gets his sheep to that place where they can rest and recharge. Sheep are never in want, in part because the shepherd sees to it that they have the provisions they need in the pasture and stream. And because of the shepherd's provision, the sheep have more than enough.

We all need gas in the tank. Otherwise, we will not get very far. For many of us, the gauges are all reading empty, but we're still waiting for the light to come on. Pretty soon you are going to sputter to a halt at the most inopportune time.

Your cup can overflow. The opportunity is available to have more than just what you need to scrape by; you can have so much that it pours over.

God has provided us with opportunities to fuel up and recharge before we run dry. He built that provision into the very fabric of creation. God created for six days and then rested on the seventh. When the Lord gave Moses the Law, it contained within it the same structure—work for six days and rest on the seventh. We now set aside the first day of the week, Sunday, as a day to focus on the Lord and reset our lives for the coming week. Yet in our rush to run wide open, we fail to use God's provision for rest. Is it any wonder that, rather than overflowing, our cup seems dry? God knows He is the source of renewal and that we desperately need to be renewed regularly. Don't miss out on the blessing that God has written into the week for us. As Isaiah says in Isaiah 40:29–31:

> He gives strength to the weary, And to him who lacks might He increases power. Though youths grow weary and tired, And vigorous young men stumble badly, Yet those who wait for the Lord Will gain new strength; They will mount up with

wings like eagles, They will run and not get tired,
They will walk and not become weary.

To me, when I am exhausted, the promise that He'll give me strength is very appealing. All I have to do is rest in Him. When your soul is weary, rest in Him. When life leaves you worn out and tired, lean on Him. He is a constant source of refreshment and renewal. Plug in to Him and let Him revive you and fill you with new strength.

You may feel your cup is empty. This week, would you allow the loving Shepherd to lead you to a place where you can refuel and recharge? Before you start sputtering, how about following the Shepherd to that sweet place where you can fill up?

Questions for Today:

1. Are you regularly spending time resting in Christ?

2. What steps are you taking to make sure you "wait upon the Lord"?

3. Do your calendar and schedule currently allow for opportunities to recharge through your time with God? If not, what steps do you need to take to see that you do?

4. How at rest do you feel at the moment? Are you consistently stressed, or do you feel at peace most of the time?

Prayer for Today:

Lord, help me make spending time with You a priority. Through my busy life, I easily find myself worn out in body and soul. I need Your help and the strength that You provide. When my soul is weary, may I find renewal in You.

Amen.

Week 5 Saturday and Sunday
You prepare a table before me in the presence of my enemies;
You have anointed my head with oil;
my cup overflows.
Psalm 23:5

G o back and review the questions from this week's daily
devotions.

1. How does your knowledge of God's ultimate victory
   change the way you respond to present fears or difficulties?

2. In what areas of your life do you feel like David as he
   faced Goliath—under-qualified, unequipped, or un-
   der-resourced?

3. What practices of rest, worship, or renewal do you
   think God is calling you to so that your cup will overflow?

4. Commit Psalm 23:5 to memory: "You prepare a table
   before me in the presence of my enemies; You have
   anointed my head with oil; my cup overflows."

Take advantage of the opportunity to refill your tank. As
you are able, go to church and gather with other believers to
worship.

Week 6

Surely goodness and lovingkindness will follow me all the days of my life,
and I will dwell in the house of the LORD forever.
Psalm 23:6

Week 6 Monday
Surely goodness and lovingkindness will follow me all the days of
my life,
and I will dwell in the house of the LORD forever.
Psalm 23:6

I was involved in a hot pursuit some years ago in a small Louisiana town. Now that may sound exciting, but unfortunately, though the police officer was aware of it, I was not.

Tonya and I had been traveling down a road marked 55 mph. Suddenly, as the highway made its way into a little village, the speed was reduced to 35 mph. Somehow, I missed that important detail. The patrolman did not. As I sped by, unaffected by the speed limit change and still going well over the 55 mph, the chase was on.

Lights came on; the siren wailed.

I missed it all. For several miles, in fact.

It was a busy road filled with plenty of other cars. I kept the hammer down, moving in and out the traffic at 55 mph, all while the officer attempted to play catch-up. I was so distracted by all the other drivers on the road that I remained completely oblivious to the lights pursuing me.

Let's just say that when I became aware, I pulled over and rolled down the window; the officer was unamused. There was no way I was getting out of that ticket.

We know what it is like to be pursued. Sometimes what chases us makes us fretful or distressed. David understands that in the Psalms. Enemies pursued him more than occasionally. You'd think that David would write something like this: "God has been good to me, even as my enemies have pursued me all the days of my life."

David's focus isn't on the trouble behind him, but the Lord's active love and care that has been in hot pursuit. Wherever he goes, he finds that the goodness of God meets him there.

There were seasons he may have initially missed it, distracted temporarily by the issues of the day that he was facing. Or maybe the people he had difficulties with temporarily consumed his attention. Yet, there it was, day in and day out, the lovingkindness of God. God's purposeful kindness and goodness to him are there, serving as a constant reminder of the continual care he is receiving from the Good Shepherd.

The Shepherd makes it a point to pursue His sheep. No matter how much they roam, the Shepherd goes out after His sheep. As such, His care pursues them as they roam. They don't have to chase His care; the care chases them.

I am reminded again just what that lovingkindness looks like. We are all sheep who have gone astray. We rebel against the Shepherd and choose our own path—a path that will lead us to our ultimate doom. But God doesn't give up on us. Instead, He pursues us. Romans 5:8 reminds us, "God demonstrates His own love toward us, in that while we were yet sinners, Christ died for us." That is the ultimate act of lovingkindness. While we are running from Him, He pursues us and lays down His life for us. The Shepherd shows how much He loves us by giving His very life up for His sheep. That is amazing love and kindness.

Trouble and trials always seem to be in our rearview mirror. Every time we look back, it is like the famous scene from Jurassic Park. We're the driver of the Jeep, and the Tyrannosaurus is right behind us.

Rest assured, though, it isn't the dinosaur that deserves our attention. It is menacing, big, and distracting but isn't a genuine threat. There are far better things pursuing us. God's constant kindness and compassion are in hot pursuit. We may not immediately see them, but they are there. They were there when He died for us. They are there as He continues to pursue us, even as we wander.

Think for a moment about how much God has cared for you this week. Think of the times when, in the middle of something troubling, God has shown up and revealed His tremendous love for you. Maybe it was an encouraging word that came at just the instant you needed it most. Maybe it was that near miss that you avoided for no other reason but that the Lord intervened and slowed you down or allowed you to miss that turn. Maybe it was that extra blessing that came out of nowhere to meet an impending need. You weren't sure how you were going to make it, but God knew and provided what you needed out of His lovingkindness. You didn't have to chase any of those things. He chased you.

Wherever you go as His sheep, you can be sure that His abundant and active love and compassion are in hot pursuit. Look back, slow down, pull over, and see how the Good Shepherd will bless you and will show you how much He loves you today.

Questions for Today:

1. What are some ways you see God actively loving and caring for you today?

2. Is it easier to see the trouble that follows us rather than the mercy and kindness that pursue us? If so, why?

3. What are some things you can do to bring His kindness and care into focus daily?

Prayer for Today:

Lord, help me see the ways You are taking care of me today. Open my eyes and help me shift my gaze from the trouble and trials around me and onto the provisions and blessings that I experience from Your hand each and every day. Let me be a person who recognizes and appreciates the way You pursue me with Your love and mercy.

Amen.

Week 6 Tuesday

*Surely goodness and lovingkindness will follow me all the days of
my life,
and I will dwell in the house of the LORD forever.*
Psalm 23:6

S ome people have catchphrases. You know the person by the
line.

"I'll be back." —The Terminator

"Life is like a box of chocolates." —Forrest Gump

"How you doin'?" —Joey Tribbiani

"What's up, doc?" —Bugs Bunny

You get the picture. You know people by particular things
they have said.

I've got a dear friend who has a few phrases people know him
by. "Great day in the morning!" is one of those. If I hear it, or if
I hear someone quoting it, I know exactly who it came from.

If you've been around me very much, you'll know I have a
phrase like that too. I say it all the time. I mean it when I say it.

"God is good . . . all the time, and all the time . . . God is good!"

I love that statement. What a powerful truth to exclaim! One
day, when this life is over and I'm laid to rest, I hope those words
will mark my headstone.

I believe in the truth and power of the statement.

God has been so incredibly good to me. Incredibly good is
the only way to describe it. His goodness has been far beyond

anything I could have deserved or possibly imagined. He has been good all the time.

Even in those seasons when I couldn't immediately see it, He was still good. He has blessed me beyond my wildest dreams. Let's pull back the curtain and let me show you just how good He has been.

I am currently alive as I write this, and that is no small feat. He gave me breath as I awoke this morning, and I'm still enjoying that. Countless people could not experience that today, but I can. That is a blessing—the blessing of another moment.

The Lord gifted me with an incredible family. My wife is the love of my life and is the perfect companion for me. A guy like me doesn't deserve a woman like that, but God provided the woman of my dreams. I have three outstanding children. They have brought such joy to my life watching them grow and become who God designed them to be.

I have a roof over my head and a place to call home. It isn't Buckingham Palace, but it is a treasure to me. Laughter and wonderful, deep conversations fill our home. As much as I love traveling, I love coming home.

I have a great job. I have served wonderful churches and worked alongside some of the most amazing and talented people imaginable. I get to share the journey of faith with wonderful friends.

Now, none of those things is perfect—except for my wife, of course. I am alive and breathing, but there are health challenges. I have an incredible family, but they are perfectly imperfect, like

I am. There have been struggles and trials as kids have grown. I have a wonderful home, but it requires a lot of maintenance and upkeep because, like me, it has some years on it. I have worked at some wonderful churches with amazing people, but there have been plenty of struggles, heartbreak, and missteps along the way.

And yet God has been so good to me in all of it! My life isn't perfect, but it is so very good thanks to the grace of God.

Your life doesn't look like mine, even if you are part of my family. Your experiences will differ from mine, as will your home, your work, and your life. But God is still so very good to you if you belong to Him.

You are alive today, or else you wouldn't be reading this. What a gift that is! Everything else is icing on the cake. You may not have everything you want or everything you once had. You may struggle with your job, be looking for a home, or be wrestling with your health. But right now, you are alive! You can laugh, love, cry, think, at least for another moment. That is a gift. Surely goodness and lovingkindness have been following you all the days of your life.

I don't know what today will hold for you. The struggles you will deal with today will be a mystery to me. I couldn't tell you the highs and lows of the next few hours for you. But I can tell you with absolute certainty this inescapable truth for you, whoever and wherever you are. God is good . . . all the time.

JOHN A. MATTHEWS

While my story is unique to me, the source of the goodness isn't. The Shepherd's goodness and lovingkindness are pursuing you too. Where do you see it in your own life today?

There was a song I learned as a kid (it's probably better that I am typing this rather than singing it):

> *God is so good. God is so good. God is so good. He's so good to me.*[1]

Yes, He is! And remember, He's good to you too!

Questions for Today:

1. What are five ways that you see God is good today?

2. How can you express the goodness of God to those around you who may struggle?

3. How can you be intentional today in giving thanks to God for His goodness and lovingkindness toward you?

4. Who can you tell today that you are thankful for God putting them in your life?

---

1. Traditional gospel hymn, author unknown

Prayer for Today:

Lord, You are so good to me. I neglect to consider just how wonderful You've been to me throughout my life, but I want to express my gratitude right now. Thank You for how good You've been to me. I don't deserve it, but You have given me more than I ever imagined possible. Help me have a heart of thanks in those moments when things are difficult, and help me see Your goodness in those times too.

Amen.

Week 6 Wednesday
Surely goodness and lovingkindness will follow me all the days of
my life,
and I will dwell in the house of the LORD forever.
Psalm 23:6

S ometimes the journey is tough. Sometimes the road is
rocky. You can become weary, frustrated, and discouraged
along the way. Hang on! There is joy up ahead. You just have to
keep walking until the end.

When my son Andrew and I took the Grand Canyon hike,
instead of going from the south rim to the river and back, we
traveled from rim to rim. Entering the canyon from the north,
we planned to stay three days in the canyon before hiking out
on the fourth day. I didn't think it was possible, but it was
somehow even hotter than the hike I had made with Alex those
years prior. It was miserably hot. The heat was so intense, we
couldn't sleep at night; we just lay there in the open and prayed a
breeze would blow. It didn't. The heat attacked us oppressively.
Two nights in and we could stand no more. Even though the
road was long, we had to find relief and find it soon. We were
determined to exit the canyon a day earlier than planned to
escape the heat. Our legs had given out, and the packs we were
carrying were increasingly heavy with every step. As Andrew
and I made our way up the last stretch, we navigated a series of
switchbacks. We'd give our all to get to one side, rest a minute,
then traverse up the next section. Back and forth. Slower and

slower each time. With every step, we were closer to the top, but each step moved our weary legs up steep inclines of the winding, seemingly never-ending path.

We understood what was ahead. Ice-cold sodas awaited. Even better, when we got to the car, we were heading to the Big Texan Steak Ranch, home of the 72-ounce steak! Oh, we didn't plan on eating the steak, but we knew it was ready for us if we chose to. Getting there required us to keep moving until we got out of the scorching canyon.

We were *so* excited when we reached the top. With the end in sight, we began celebrating. We were shouting even before we got to the trailhead. Our legs couldn't do much jumping, but our spirits sure were. We knew relief was just ahead. We were almost there!

With only a hundred yards to go, a family spotted us making our ascent. This family was from another area and didn't speak our language. They may not have known what we were saying, but they definitely understood what we were feeling. As we took those last steps out of the canyon, we *all* celebrated together. We couldn't understand a word they were saying, and I'm pretty sure they couldn't understand anything we were saying, but all of us rejoiced together that Andrew and I had completed the journey.

There are seasons when the road is incredibly tough. The weight of life bears down on you. It is inevitable; there will be times when your soul feels drained, and you can't seem to find any relief or rest. You may feel like all you are doing is climbing uphill on a never-ending path. Don't give up. The joy is still up ahead.

James, the brother of Jesus, says in James 1:12, "Blessed is a man who perseveres under trial; for once he has been approved, he will receive the crown of life which the Lord has promised to those who love Him." You may not be done with the road yet, and there may be hard days still ahead, but you can start the celebration. Joy is up ahead. When we have finished this journey, we will get to dwell in the house of the Lord forever! And what a collective celebration it will be!

Today, if you feel like throwing in the towel, don't give up. Keep walking. Press on. Rest is up ahead.

Questions for Today:

1. Would you say you are in a season when life's road is difficult or easy?

2. What can you do to focus on the joy ahead over the struggles now?

3. Do you find it difficult to rejoice when times are tough, even though you know joy awaits ahead? Why or why not?

4. What is one thing God has taught you as you have walked down a rough road?

Prayer for Today:

Lord, help me trust You wherever You lead me. When I have an abundance, help me remember it wasn't because of what I have earned or achieved. In times of struggle, help me remember I am not forgotten or neglected. Help me keep my eyes fixed on my Shepherd, who provides for me in the grassy places and on the rocky hillside, on hard roads and in easy steps. Help me trust His provision.

Amen.

Surely goodness and lovingkindness will follow me all the days of
my life,
and I will dwell in the house of the LORD forever.
Psalm 23:6

W e long for home.

We've heard it said a million times. There is no place like home. Home is where the heart is. As cliché as those sound, they are absolutely true. A desire for home is entrenched deep within us. Even for those from broken homes, there is a longing for a true home woven into the fabric of our DNA.

Home is more than an address, more than wood or brick. Home is more than square footage, paint schemes, or floor plans. At the end of it all, home is about presence. Home is about the who more than the where and what.

Here, in the last words of Psalm 23, we hear David talking about a day when he will dwell in the house of the Lord forever. It is the joyous finishing touches on a portrait he has been beautifully painting. It is the crescendo of the song he has been singing. This is the last exclamation point in this poetic piece. The height of the stanza declares: There is a day coming when I will be in His house for all eternity!

Our natural tendency here is to assume that David is longing for heaven. The final word directing us to the eternal life God's people will enjoy. After all our labor and trials in this world, there will be a heavenly home we get to inhabit, an eternal reward we will experience. While there may be some of that idea here, I think that misses what David is really saying. He isn't looking forward to an unending place; he's looking forward to an uninterrupted presence. He was excited about the prospect of being in God's presence forever.

In David's day, there weren't churches on every corner. The temple hadn't yet been built for them to gather to worship and offer sacrifices. In those days, there was the tabernacle. While in the wilderness, God had instructed Moses to build a tent that would travel with the people. It was a portable sanctuary. God's presence was there in that tabernacle. Where the people went, the tent went, and God was with them. That tabernacle—the house of the Lord—was a tangible reminder of God being present. He resided in that tent. No, the tent did not confine Him within its walls, but His glory filled that place like no other.

By the time we get to Psalm 23, there are actually two tabernacles. The original one, built in Moses's day, was in Gibeon. David, though, had another tabernacle put together. In this tabernacle of David, the ark of the covenant resided. It was in this house of the Lord that David loved so well.

He will say in Psalm 122:1: "I was glad when they said to me, 'Let's go to the house of the LORD.'"

In Psalm 27:4, David says, "One thing I have asked from the LORD, that I shall seek: That I may dwell in the house of the LORD all the days of my life, To behold the beauty of the LORD And to meditate in His temple."

The house of the Lord was an actual place, but through the years, for David, it was less about a physical address and more about the One associated with it. David just loved the Lord. And with every fiber of his being, he wanted to be in His presence all the time. David wanted to see the Lord's beauty, to stand in awe of His glory. While David enjoyed the times he had the opportunity to be there at the tabernacle, those moments were always too brief. David could go to the house of the Lord, but he couldn't live there.

God is present with us all the time. We understand that He does not reside in church buildings or at a physical address. However, we also understand that although He is present, we cannot fully experience His presence in this life. We can't see His presence or hear His voice audibly. David is reminding us that there is a day coming when that dynamic will forever change. We won't get to just visit His presence, get a glimpse of it now and then, but rather, we will live in His presence. Continually for all time. We will see Him as He is. What a great day that will be!

Wherever you go today, He is present with you, even if you can't see Him with your physical eyes. And as you remind yourself of that truth, let it encourage you that the best days are just ahead, when you will see Him face to face!

Questions for Today:

1. When you think of home, what comes to mind?

2. What about being in the "house of the Lord" brings joy to you?

3. How does the promise of being in the Lord's presence forever affect how you live today?

4. How can we prepare now for dwelling there later?

Prayer for Today:

Father, we look forward to the day when we will be in Your presence for all time. Help us hold fast to that hope as we look for that coming day. Thank You for the promise of what is yet to come.

Amen.

Surely goodness and lovingkindness will follow me all the days of my life,
and I will dwell in the house of the LORD forever.
Psalm 23:6

I t is one thing to say it. It is another thing to actually believe it.

David makes a bold statement. I will dwell in the house of the Lord forever.

Not I hope I will.

Not I probably will.

But this is a definitive statement. I *will* dwell in the house of the Lord forever. There was no doubt in his mind about it. It was a settled reality in his life. He knew it was true. He believed it.

What about you?

You can know spiritual-sounding answers and still not rest on biblical truth. Plenty of people know this psalm and other Bible verses that affirm that those who trust in Christ will lack nothing they need. Yet, those same people live stressed-out lives as they face situations where that truth is put to the test. Their lips say they know it, but their lives say they don't believe it.

When the kids were small, and they were learning to swim, I saw this very thing played out with each one. It was an illustration of the tension between knowledge and belief. I'd be in the pool with each child. The instructions were simple. Put your arms out, head in the water, kick those legs, and swim to me. I was literally just a foot or so in front of them. Each one knew I loved them. They knew I would not let them drown. They knew I was right there to grab them if they needed help. And each of them still did the same thing. They freaked out. None would keep their heads in the water. Each panicked and splashed around until they could reach my outstretched arms.

Every time.

They knew I would not let them go under. But none of them swam like it. If they couldn't see me there or feel my outstretched arm, the fear overtook their faith. All they saw was the water and not their loving father.

Fear can paralyze us. If we worry about the how and when of God's provision, we can end up missing out on where God wants to lead us and what He wants to show us. Rather than stress over the needs, trust what you know; He will provide, and you won't be lacking in anything.

Jesus spoke about this in what we call the Sermon on the Mount. It's found in the Gospel of Matthew, chapters 5 through 7. Go check it out.

In the middle of this incredible teaching, Jesus speaks to a reality so many of us experience. In Matthew 6, Jesus addresses the anxiety we often feel when we consider the needs we face. Jesus talks about the common needs we think we have, the ones most clear to us—our need for food and clothing. We all need these things to survive. But I think Jesus was using those basic

JOHN A. MATTHEWS

elements of need to express a much grander truth. If He can meet those needs, surely He will meet the other needs too.

It's a perfect illustration. He directs their attention to some birds flying around. Small, relatively insignificant birds that, had Jesus not called them out, probably no one would have noticed. He reminds the people that those little birds aren't freaking out about what they are going to eat. God provides for them. If God provides for little birds, who nobody even pays much attention to, wouldn't He provide even more for our needs? After all, while God does love all His creation, He loves humankind more than the birds. He has a special relationship with people.

Driving the point even further, Jesus points to some beautiful lilies. Back in the day, King Solomon had everything. He had all the riches and resources you could obtain. He was a sharp-dressed man. Jesus says that even King Solomon didn't dress as well as those lilies. Here is the thing: Flowers don't stress about what they look like or what they are going to wear. God's got them covered . . . literally. God provides.

Flowers are here today and gone tomorrow, and as lovely as they are, they fall lower on the scale than we do. If He takes care of the lilies, He will definitely take care of us. God loves the birds and the lilies, and takes care of both, so they lack nothing. But neither birds nor flowers are His sheep. We are His sheep, and the Shepherd cares for us in a way that far exceeds that of the birds and flowers. If they don't worry, neither should we. I'm sure you know God will provide for you, so now trust that He always will.

Today, temptation may lead you to stress or worry about a need you have. You know God is aware. He sees the situation better than even you do. You know He loves you and cares for you. Instead of coming undone over it, trust Jesus. You may not see yet how He is going to walk you through this, but you know He will. Trust Him. He cares for you and will provide for you, now and forever.

If you are one of His sheep, be confident in what is coming!

Questions for Today:

1. What needs are you most worried about today?

2. When facing those needs, what can keep you from becoming stressed out?

3. How will you express trust and not just knowledge in your relationship with Christ today?

Prayer for Today:

Lord, help me live a life of boldness and confidence. Help me trust You even when I can't quite see how You are going to provide. Thank You for always meeting my needs. You move in ways I don't expect to meet needs I didn't even know I had. Your care for my life is amazing!

Amen.

Week 6 Saturday and Sunday
Surely goodness and lovingkindness will follow me all the days of my life,
and I will dwell in the house of the LORD forever.
Psalm 23:6

G o back and review the questions from this week's daily devotions.

1. How will you slow down this week and experience the lovingkindness of God in real-time?

2. When you are looking in the "rear-view mirror," are you focusing on the troubles behind you or the goodness of God that is pursuing you? How can adjusting your focus impact the peace and rest you will experience this week?

3. What are some expressions of God's kindness that you experienced this week because goodness and lovingkindness were pursuing you and you didn't have to chase after them?

4. Commit Psalm 23:6 to memory: "Surely goodness and lovingkindness will follow me all the days of my life, and I will dwell in the house of the LORD forever."

That's a wrap! You have made your way through Psalm 23. You know it by heart. What better way to celebrate than to gather with some folks and give thanks to the Lord, for He is good. Let this weekend be a time when you joyously proclaim, "The Lord is *My Shepherd*!"

About the Author

John A. Matthews is a pastor and writer whose work explores the intersection of faith and everyday life. Drawing from years of pastoral ministry and a deep love for Scripture, he writes devotionals, reflections, and stories that invite readers to slow down, listen closely, and notice the quiet ways God is at work. Through his writing, John seeks to offer words that are honest, grace-filled, and rooted in the belief that faith is formed not only in the extraordinary, but in the ordinary moments of life. You can visit John online at www.jmwriting.com.

www.ingramcontent.com/pod-product-compliance
Lightning Source LLC
Chambersburg PA
CBHW071754090426
42737CB00012B/1817